The
BATTLE
of the
HEDGEROWS

The
BATTLE
of the
HEDGEROWS

Bradley's First Army in Normandy, June–July 1944

Leo Daugherty

Ian Allan
PUBLISHING

British Library Cataloguing in Publication Data:
A catalogue record for this book is available
from the British Library

ISBN 0 7110 2832 X

First published in the UK in 2001 by
Ian Allan Publishing

an imprint of Ian Allan Publishing Ltd
Terminal House
Shepperton, Surrey
TW17 8AS
England

1 3 5 7 9 8 6 4 2

Editorial and design:
Brown Partworks Ltd
8 Chapel Place
Rivington Street
London
EC2A 3DQ
UK

Editors: Peter Darman, Tony Hall
Picture research: Antony Shaw
Design: Mike Lebihan
Maps: Darren Awuah
Production: Matt Weyland

Printed in Hong Kong

TO THE AMERICAN SOLDIERS WHO
FOUGHT IN THE "BLOODY *BOCAGE*"
IN WORLD WAR II

CONTENTS

KEY TO MAPS

Military units – types

(box with X)	infantry
(box with parallelogram)	armoured
(box with parallelogram outline)	motorized infantry/ panzergrenadier
(box with arcs)	parachute/airborne

Military units – size

Marking	Size
XXXXX	army group/front
XXXX	army
XXX	corps
XX	division
III	regiment
II	battalion
I	company
•••	platoon

Military unit colours

Colour	Nation
(grey)	German
(dark grey)	US

Military movement

→ US attack arrow

Geographical symbols

——	road
•	urban area
(shape)	urban area/building
(shape)	trees
- - - -	track
(burst)	hill
(shape)	marsh
——	river
-•-•-•-	railway

LIST OF MAPS

INTRODUCTION

The period following the Allied landings in Normandy has been the subject of intense debate among military historians as to the failure of the US First Army to break out from the *bocage* country in the immediate aftermath of the landings on 6 June 1944. This book hopes to illustrate how Allied planning failed to take into account not only the terrain factors, but the Wehrmacht's ability to utilize the terrain to its defensive advantage. *The Battle of the Hedgerows* is an in-depth account of the seven weeks that followed the American landings at Omaha and Utah beaches, and of the war of attrition that followed as German resistance stiffened.

While General Dwight D. Eisenhower and his staff at SHAEF (Supreme Headquarters Allied Expeditionary Force) had hoped that American and British forces would be able to advance rapidly inland and take advantage of their overwhelming superiority in both men and materiel over those of the German forces on the Cotentin Peninsula, a combination of rather poor intelligence and over-ambitious objectives culminated in a near disaster for Lieutenant-General Omar N. Bradley's First Army. As a result of this failure to advance quickly inland, the battle for the *bocage* developed into a bloody stalemate that disrupted the Allied timetables for a speedy victory in France, and enabled the Wehrmacht to reorganize hastily and strengthen its forces.

This book will examine the fight for the *bocage* against the plans laid out by SHAEF and the initial landings in Normandy, and how the failure to detect German defences culminated in the war of attrition that followed. As will be seen in the fight for the *bocage*, the tank-infantry team came into its own as American and German infantrymen fought small, set-piece battles for control of the hedgerows. Indeed, this battle was one waged and won by infantry squads slugging it out from hedgerow to hedgerow, and the fight for the *bocage* country serves both as an important lesson for today's infantry, as well as a reminder that World War II was ultimately an infantryman's war.

CHAPTER I:

PRE-INVASION PLANS AND OBJECTIVES

What Operation Overlord planners knew of the *bocage* country. The organization and command structure of the German Army in Normandy in 1944.

In order to examine in greater detail the stalemate that occurred after the D-Day landings, it is necessary to examine the pre-D-Day Allied strategy and German defensive strategy adopted to counter the landings if the invasion were to occur in Normandy. For it is in both the offensive and defensive plans that the battle in the *bocage* countryside occurred.

The fighting in France's *bocage* country had its origins in the initial planning for Overlord. Indeed, when Major-General Ray Barker (Deputy Chief-of-Staff to General Dwight D. Eisenhower and formerly head of the initial American planning group) and chief British planner Major-General J.E. Sinclair, set out in late 1942 and early 1943 to examine potential landing sites for a massive landing in Northwest Europe, the terrain beyond the beachhead was given little if any consideration. After an exhaustive study of potential landing sites, both Generals Barker and Sinclair reported that given the overall strategy of the campaign and initial operational goals of securing adequate port facilities,

■ *Left:* **Successful amphibious warfare needed specialist equipment, and this DUKW amphibious truck and the US Navy LST (Landing Ship, Tank) it is embarking on prior to D-Day were state-of-the art in 1944.**

and in order to facilitate an area capable of sustaining a rapid build up to compete with that of the enemy, both Caen and the Cotentin Peninsula were agreed upon as the area of main attack. While the planners concluded that this involved an acceptable risk as to the extension of its already tenuous lines of communication and supply, they nonetheless agreed that the risks were "acceptable" only if "it were considered essential to build up a large force west of and protected by the River Seine".[1]

After several operational revisions during the early months of 1943, the basic plan for a landing in Northwest Europe was given tentative approval by the Combined Commanders on 1 March, and served as the basis for all subsequent planning for a cross-Channel attack and the initial operating guidelines, codenamed Skyscraper. This plan called for simultaneous landings on the Caen and east Cotentin beaches with four divisions in the initial assault wave and six in the waves to follow. The plan also called for an additional force of 18 Commando units (each with about 700 men) for special assault missions behind enemy lines, and for four airborne divisions to disrupt German attempts at reinforcing the landing areas with reserves. After the initial forces secured the beachhead, as well as the port of Cherbourg, an additional landing might be necessary so as to facilitate the overland attack. The landing forces were then to continue northeast towards Antwerp and secure the area between the Pas-de-Calais and

■ *Above:* An Italian tank is checked for boobytraps after the US Army's first major battle with the Axis at the Kasserine Pass, Tunisia, in February 1943. America's new army was quick to learn from its defeat at the hands of Rommel in this battle.

the Ruhr.[2] In essence, the Allies were to conduct a massive sweep through Northwest Europe, liberating France and the Low Countries, and drive into the heart of Germany. The campaign initiated on 6 June 1944 was to be a mobile one, utilizing the Allies' preponderance of armour and mechanized assets, as well as their ability to resupply rapidly through their superior logistical infrastructure.

After numerous revisions to the original Skyscraper Plan, Overlord, as the overall landing plan was now called, focused upon the Caen-Cotentin Peninsula areas as the sites for the main and secondary landings, and it is here that Allied planners set about to draft their final plans not only for the invasion of Europe, but for the defeat of the Wehrmacht (German armed forces) and of Nazi Germany itself. While

British and American intelligence officials gathered reports and intercepted German radio traffic through Ultra (the codename for reading top-secret German teleprinter massages) on German strength in the Normandy sector, the terrain, specifically Normandy's *bocage* country, where the US First Army under the command of Lieutenant-General Omar N. Bradley would have to fight, was given slight consideration by the commanders with no mention given to the men who would fight there. In his postwar memoirs, Lieutenant-General Bradley wrote that the Allies had hoped to avoid a bloody war of attrition if at all possible. General Bradley maintained that: "From the moment we started on Overlord planning, I was determined that we must avoid at all costs those pitfalls that might bog down our advance and lead

■ *Below:* The American soldiers that faced the Afrika Korps in Tunisia in 1943 were green, and paid for their inexperience with defeat.

us into the trench warfare of World War I."[3] He added that mobility was the key to achieving a rapid decision in France as it had been in Tunisia in 1943:

"We had fought a fast war of movement in the Tunisian campaign where the terrain mitigated against us, and I was convinced those tactics could be duplicated in a blitz across France. With the mobility and firepower we had amassed in both British and American divisions we could easily outpoint and outrun the Germans in an open war of movement."[4]

■ *Left:* Three days before D-Day and their landing on Utah Beach, men of the US 4th Infantry Division march to their ships through the empty civilian-free streets of Torquay in Devon just after dawn. By 22 June these soldiers would be assaulting the bastion of German-held Cherbourg.

Despite Bradley's opinion that the Americans had to achieve a rapid breakout of the beachhead and move swiftly inland, the fact remained that the First Army had neither prepared for a stiffened German resistance nor inhospitable terrain, two factors that they would confront in Normandy before

they could conduct the type of campaign called for in Operation Overlord's overall strategic aim for the invasion.

It is a well-known fact that prior to the D-Day landings American and British planners knew of the *bocage* country, and the inhibiting characteristics in conducting combat operations over terrain that favoured the defender. Whereas the terrain in the British and Canadian sectors (Field Marshal Sir Bernard L. Montgomery's Twenty-First Army Group) favoured the conduct of mechanized operations, due to its open countryside, pastures and rolling hills, the area assigned to American forces was a maze of broken and uneven terrain features surrounded by small plots of land enclosed by thick hedgerows that the French called *bocage*. Almost as soon as American forces began the advance inland from the beaches in Normandy, they ran into the first of what was to prove a huge series of hedgerows or half-earthen embankments made up of both hedges and packed earth, varying in thickness from 300mm to 1.2m (1 to 4 feet) and in heights that ranged from 900mm to 4.5m (3 to 15 feet). Growing out of these hedgerows were small trees, bushes and vines that impeded both vision and movement. These hedgerows surrounded each field and broke the terrain into compartments that in turn inhibited swift mobility. Each hedgerow had an opening so as to allow the passage of livestock and people onto the narrow roads that straddled them. While there were some paved roads that ran through the First Army's sector, the majority of roads in the *bocage* country were secondary, unpaved dirt roads that were surrounded on both sides by heavy vegetation that further inhibited movement of men and materiel.

As one historian wrote, the military characteristics of this hedgerow territory were obvious:

"The hedgerows in each field provide excellent cover and concealment to the defender and present a formidable obstacle to the attacker. Numerous adjoining fields can be organized to form a natural defensive position echeloned in depth. The thick vegetation provides excellent camouflage and limits the deployment of combat units. The hedgerows also restrict observation, making the use of heavy calibre direct fire weapons almost impossible and hampering the adjustment of indirect artillery fire. Consequently, anyone occupying a high place that afforded good fields of observation and a clear view of the surrounding countryside would have a distinct advantage . . . "[5]

In addition, as both American and German planners discovered as the battle in the *bocage* took shape, the paved roads that existed in the First Army's sector became vital to the success or failure of the Allied advance inland towards Carentan and St-Lô. Whoever controlled St-Lô could retain his hold over much of the road network in the *bocage* country, and thus prevent or facilitate the advance of the Allies.[6]

Given the fact that the summer of 1944 was perhaps the wettest since 1900, the area west of Carentan and specifically in the *bocage* country had been transformed into a quagmire. This in turn restricted the movement of American vehicles and made cross-country movement virtually impossible. Added to the low visibility and cloud ceilings that now covered the Normandy battlefield, American soldiers would fight the German Army in the *bocage* largely without the benefit of close air support from its vast arsenal of fighter-bombers. Added to the problems of resupply, due to the same storms that grounded its air support, the

American soldier was forced to take on a German Army that had had the time to position itself expertly into the *bocage* country of Normandy.

The German Army in Normandy

The German Army that faced the US First Army in the *bocage* country was a mixture of reservists, recruits, foreign conscripts and battle-hardened veterans. The overall German commander in France during and immediately after D-Day was Field Marshal Gerd von

Rundstedt, Commander-in-Chief of the West. Immediately under Field Marshal von Rundstedt were two subordinate commanders, Field Marshal Erwin Rommel, the famed "Desert Fox", who commanded Army Group B (the Netherlands and Loire sectors), and Colonel-General Johannes Blaskowitz, in command of Army Group G (the River Loire, Spanish frontier, Mediterranean coast and Alps sectors).

Field Marshal Rommel's Army Group B consisted of two armies, comprising eight army corps headquarters, 24 infantry divisions and five Luftwaffe field divisions. The two armies were the Fifteenth and Seventh. The Fifteenth Army, commanded by Colonel-General Hans von Salmuth, an experienced field commander with great tactical and operational acumen, consisted of four army headquarters, five infantry divisions and two Luftwaffe field divisions at the front; and seven infantry divisions and one Luftwaffe field division in reserve. The

■ *Below:* **A DUKW of the 462nd Amphibious Truck Company drives ashore during training off the Cornish coast in March 1944. The southwest of England was the holding area for the US First Army.**

other army was the Seventh, commanded by Colonel-General Friedrich von Dollman, and consisted of three army headquarters; five frontline infantry divisions; two infantry divisions in reserve, the 91st Airborne Division, and later two parachute divisions. It should be mentioned that the parachute divisions provided the stiffest resistance during the fighting in the *bocage*.

The German Army in the West 1944
Commander in Chief,
German Forces West
Field Marshal Gerd von Rundstedt

Army Group B
Field Marshal Erwin Rommel

Fifteenth Army
Colonel-General Hans von Salmuth
Frontline Formations
Infantry Divisions (Army)
47th, 49th, 70th, 344th, 711th
Luftwaffe Field Divisions (Air Force) 17th, 18th

Reserve Divisions
Infantry Divisions (Army)
64th, 85th, 89th, 182nd, 326th, 331st, 712th
Luftwaffe Field Divisions (Air Force) 19th

Seventh Army
   Colonel-General Friedrich
   von Dollman
In Normandy
   Infantry Divisions (Army)
   716th, 352nd, 243rd*
   Luftwaffe Field Divisions (Air
   Force)
   2 Parachute Divisions**
   91st Airborne

Reserve Divisions
   Infantry Divisions (Army)
   84th, 353rd

Channel Islands
   Infantry Divisions (Army)
   266th, 353rd

Armoured Forces in the West
   General Geyr von Schweppenburg
I SS Panzer Corps
   1st SS Panzer Division
   12th SS Panzer Division
   2nd Panzer Division,
   21st Panzer Division
   116th Panzer Division

* Not at full strength during the invasion on 6 June 1944.
** Added to the Order of Battle after the Normandy landings.

■ *Above:* Opening the way into the *bocage* country, troops, probably of the **101st Airborne**, march through Carentan – the first major French town to be liberated by the First Army, on **12 June**, the same day on which units from Utah and Omaha beachheads linked up.

■ *Left:* The C-in-C-West, Field Marshal Gerd von Rundstedt, inspecting emplacements along the Atlantic Wall in August 1943 – one of the 15,000 strongpoints planned. Though officially in command of all Western defences von Rundstedt had only nominal control over Rommel's Army Group B and no control at all over the vital panzer divisions.

The entire Atlantic front from the Pyrenees to the Danish border was manned by some 60 semi-mobile infantry divisions, composed primarily of men from the Replacement Army, as the majority of battle-hardened veterans were fighting the Soviet Red Army along the Eastern Front.

As for the quality of these troops in the West, General of Infantry Hans Speidel wrote at the time that they "were, for the most part, overage and unequal to the task that was to fall to their lot. They were poorly equipped and could be compared with the type of infantry division found at the end of the First World War." General Speidel added to this criticism by saying that many of the officers and noncommissioned officers of these infantry divisions were likewise not "up to the task before them".[7]

■ *Right:* Field
Marshal Erwin
Rommel (third from
right). Serious
differences of
strategy divided
Rommel from von
Rundstedt and
further complicated
an already
confused German
command structure
in the West.

■ *Below:* One of
the founders of
Germany's airborne
forces: General
Kurt Student, seen
here inspecting
paratroopers in
France pre-D-Day.

Between 1939 and 1943, the
standard German infantry division was
organized on a triangular basis with
three regiments of three rifle battalions
each. Each of the rifle regiments had, in
addition to its 12 rifle and heavy
weapons companies, an infantry
howitzer and an antitank company
attached. Every division had an antitank
and reconnaissance battalion. Organic
artillery consisted of one regiment of
one medium (150mm howitzer) and
three light (105mm howitzer or gun)
battalions with a total armament of 48
pieces. Due to the inclusion of antitank
and reconnaissance units, the German
division was "substantially larger" than
its American counterpart, numbering
17,200 men.

After nearly four years of continuous
fighting, however, the German Army
infantry division had been drastically
reduced in strength, though it had held

its own insofar as firepower had been concerned. With more and more manpower devoted to stemming the westward push of the Red Army in the East, the Wehrmacht issued new tables of organization for the division which reduced the number of rifle battalions from three to two, though even this number was further reduced as the total strength of an infantry division by 1944 hovered around 12,769 officers and enlisted men. Wehrmacht commanders attempted to retain the fighting strength of the division through reductions in non-essential personnel, such as supply, and other non-combat-related branches. In fact, they were able to maintain a fighting strength of 75–80 percent with the 1944-Type Infantry Division.

Infantry Battalions

The reduction that occurred in the total number of rifle battalions per division was slightly alleviated with the addition of a so-called Fuesilier battalion for reconnaissance purposes. While it was organized like a rifle battalion, one company was equipped with bicycles to increase mobility. The Fuesilier battalion also had slightly more horsedrawn vehicles and some motor transport. In time, German Army commanders looked upon this unit as a seventh rifle battalion.

In addition to the reduction in the number of battalions per regiment, rifle squads and companies were also reduced in total manpower, though the number of automatic weapons per company was increased. This would have a direct effect as far as the fighting in the *bocage* was concerned, as German tactical doctrine always emphasized small infantry units equipped with maximum automatic firepower. On average, a German rifle company was able to deliver two to three times the amount of firepower offered by a comparable American company. Although the standard infantry weapon was the bolt-action Mauser 98k rifle, increased firepower at the company level came via the widespread use of the 9mm MP40 machine pistol, and light machine guns such as the MG42. Though designed to be crew-served, the MG42 in Normandy was often used with the 50-round Gurttromel basket magazine. Given the weapon's exceptional high rate of fire (up to 1000 rounds per minute), the magazine transformed its effectiveness in the *bocage*, allowing one infantryman in deep cover to fire a 50-round burst in a second or two and be clear of the area before the American rifle squad opposite knew what had hit them. In coming up against *Fallschirmjaeger* (paratroopers) around St-Lô, GIs would have also come up against the FG42 – one the few German semi-automatic rifles to see frontline service.

Rifle Companies

The average strength of a German rifle company was two officers and 140 enlisted men, whereas the American company averaged six officers and 187 enlisted men, which made the American division greater in terms of riflemen with slightly more than 12,000 combat infantrymen. With the addition of more automatic weapons per squad, however, the German division was far superior in firepower to its American or British counterpart. While equal in artillery compared to that of an American division, the German infantry division enjoyed an advantage in infantry howitzers, and a heavy superiority in automatic weapons.[8]

Older formations, such as the Luftwaffe field divisions, of which there were 20 in Normandy prior to the invasion, were likewise reorganized to meet the critical shortages in manpower. Field Marshal von Rundstedt's static, or

■ *Left:* Manning a heavily camouflaged 20mm Flak 38 antiaircraft gun, these *Fallschirmjaeger* wear the characteristic airborne helmet and second-pattern jump smock. Although after the battle for Crete in 1941 they never again flew into battle en masse, these highly trained infantrymen retained their distinctive uniforms and equipment throughout the war.

"bodenstaendige", divisions were exempted from this reorganization. These static divisions, comprised of three regiments of three battalions each, were much weaker than the reorganized divisions due to the fact that they lacked the organic reconnaissance battalion and possessed only three artillery battalions.

Undoubtedly, the best infantry units facing the Allies, specifically the Americans, were the *Fallschirmjaeger* troops. Administratively under the Luftwaffe though tactically subordinated to the army, the parachute forces had grown substantially from a pre-1944 strength of one corps to a projected force of some 100,000 men by the end of 1944. These troops were to be an élite arm and were put on an equal status with the SS units in recruiting, armament, equipment and training.

Parachute Divisions

Of these new *Fallschirmjaeger* units created in late 1943 and early 1944 were the 3rd and 5th Divisions, and the 6th Parachute Regiment (from the 2nd Parachute Division). It would be, in fact, the 3rd Division and more specifically the 6th Parachute Regiment that the Americans would face in Normandy in the *bocage* country. These parachute regiments were, according to US Army after-action reports, "first-rate fighting units".

The 3rd Parachute Division, adhering to the strength of the Type-1944 Infantry Division, comprised three regiments of three battalions each. There were separate mortar, engineer and antitank companies. While the mortar company in the 3rd Parachute Division came equipped with the standard 100mm mortars as well as the feared 105mm *Nebelwerfer* rocket launcher, the division's mortar companies had a fair number of 81mm and 120mm mortars, while the 6th

Parachute Regiment had nine of the heavy 120mm mortars attached. As for artillery, the 3rd Parachute Division had one battalion of light artillery (12 70mm howitzers). While the division had been ordered to reinforce its artillery strength with two light and one medium battalions prior to the

■ *Above:* Typical German infantry in Normandy. Camouflage gear, entrenching tools, MP40s and MG42s are all well in evidence.

Normandy landings, these measures remained unfulfilled as the Allies struck before the order could be complied with. During the fighting in the *bocage*, the 3rd Parachute Division effectively used its 12 attached 88mm antiaircraft guns as antitank weapons within the narrow confines of the battlefield.

The overall strength of the 3rd Parachute Division (15 companies) was 17,420 officers and men, while the 6th Parachute Regiment numbered some 3457 officers and enlisted men, considerably larger than the normal infantry organization. Despite being outgunned and under-manned, both

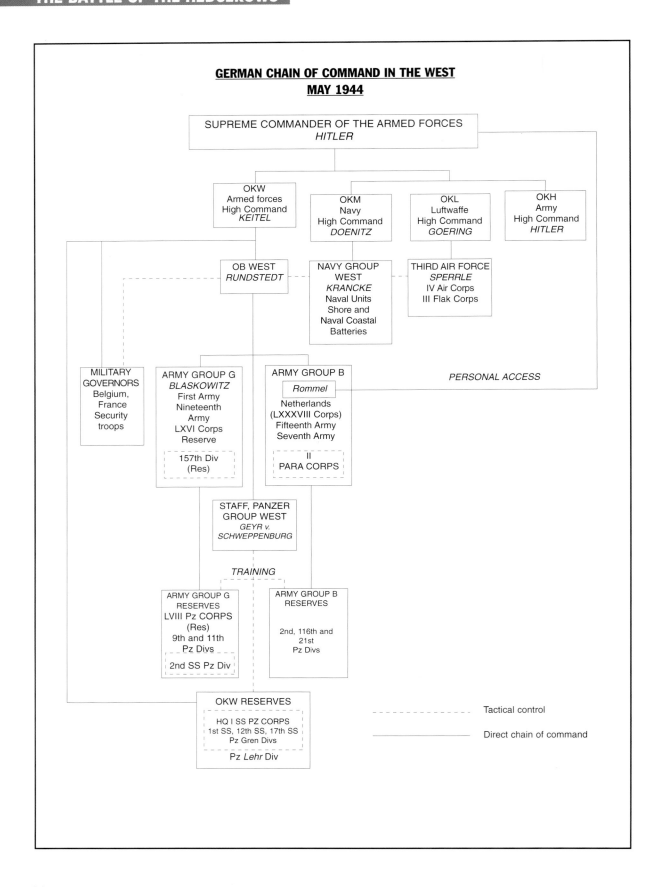

GERMAN CHAIN OF COMMAND IN THE WEST
MAY 1944

SUPREME COMMANDER OF THE ARMED FORCES
HITLER

OKW
Armed forces
High Command
KEITEL

OKM
Navy
High Command
DOENITZ

OKL
Luftwaffe
High Command
GOERING

OKH
Army
High Command
HITLER

OB WEST
RUNDSTEDT

NAVY GROUP
WEST
KRANCKE
Naval Units
Shore and
Naval Coastal
Batteries

THIRD AIR FORCE
SPERRLE
IV Air Corps
III Flak Corps

MILITARY
GOVERNORS
Belgium,
France
Security
troops

ARMY GROUP G
BLASKOWITZ
First Army
Nineteenth
Army
LXVI Corps
Reserve

157th Div
(Res)

ARMY GROUP B
Rommel
Netherlands
(LXXXVIII Corps)
Fifteenth Army
Seventh Army

II
PARA CORPS

PERSONAL ACCESS

STAFF, PANZER
GROUP WEST
*GEYR v.
SCHWEPPENBURG*

TRAINING

ARMY GROUP G
RESERVES
LVIII Pz CORPS
(Res)
9th and 11th
Pz Divs

2nd SS Pz Div

ARMY GROUP B
RESERVES

2nd, 116th and
21st
Pz Divs

OKW RESERVES

HQ I SS PZ CORPS
1st SS, 12th SS, 17th SS
Pz Gren Divs

Pz *Lehr* Div

- - - - - - - - - - Tactical control

———————— Direct chain of command

26

the 3rd Parachute Division and 6th Parachute Regiment were superior not only in numbers but in quality. Absent from the parachute formations were the ethnic Germans and Slavs that formed many of the "bodenstaendige" units. In fact, the average age of the members of these élite *Fallschirmjaeger* formations was 18, and the men had fighting morale considered to be unshaken in the wake of the erosion of Germany's military fortunes.

Like the 1st *Leibstandarte* and 12th *Hitlerjugend* Divisions of the Waffen-SS, both the 3rd Parachute Division and 6th Parachute Regiment were much better armed than the regular Wehrmacht formations. Both parachute formations had "twice as many light machine guns as the infantry division's rifle companies. The heavy weapons companies with 12 heavy machine guns and six medium mortars each were also superior in firepower to those found in the army units."[9] The one major weakness in the parachute units was the perennial problem of motor transport. Possessing only 70 trucks of all types and models, the *Fallschirmjaegers* suffered from the same lack of mobility that would hinder Field Marshal von Rundstedt's infantry from effectively blocking American breakthroughs during the *bocage* fighting.

Panzergrenadier Units

The last type of German unit at Normandy, and one which the Americans would face in the *bocage*, were the panzergrenadiers or mechanized infantry. By US Army definition panzergrenadier units were infantry divisions with organic tank battalions, some armoured personnel carriers, and some self-propelled artillery. At the time of the Normandy landings, the only panzergrenadier formation in the West was the 17th SS Panzergrenadier

Division *Goetz von Berlichingen*, whose strength had been centred around its six rifle battalions, a tank battalion of 37 Sturmgeschütz assault guns, and an antitank battalion of one company equipped with nine 75mm and three 76.2mm guns. The 17th SS Panzergrenadier Division also had an armoured reconnaissance battalion of six companies and an antiaircraft battalion equipped with the much-feared 88mm antiaircraft gun.

The Numbers Question

At the time of the Normandy landings, OB West's strength comprised six army and three SS panzer divisions. Personnel strength of the army divisions ranged from 12,768 (9th Panzer) to 16,466 (2nd Panzer). The SS divisions, which had six instead of the standard four infantry battalions, varied in personnel strength from 17,590 (9th SS Panzer) to 21,386 (1st SS Panzer). Despite this variance in personnel strength the German panzer divisions were larger than their American counterparts, though they had fewer tanks. Both the SS and Army panzer divisions were armed with the Mk IV 75mm medium tank and the superb Mk V Panther with its deadly long 75mm gun. Other tanks found in the panzer divisions varied from the Mk III (50mm guns) and Mk III and Mk IV (assault guns) Sturmgeschütz (75mm guns). In almost every instance, despite the superiority in design and armament, the German panzer divisions, both army and SS, were severely under-equipped and undermanned due largely to the drain in manpower and materiel by units on the Eastern Front.

The organization of the Army panzer divisions included, in addition to the two regiments (four battalions) of infantry and one tank regiment, a self-propelled antitank battalion (armed

mostly with assault guns), an armoured reconnaissance battalion, a towed antiaircraft battalion, and an artillery regiment with one light self-propelled battalion, one light towed battalion and one medium towed battalion. The only difference with the SS and army divisions was the additional towed light artillery battalion found in the former.[10]

As General of Infantry[11] Hans Speidel wrote, "the armoured divisions had not been brought up to full strength, and their training was unfinished. They were short of tried officers and of materiel. But the fighting potential of the armoured divisions was higher than that of the stationary infantry divisions, although it was only about 30 percent of the 1940 and 1941 standards of such divisions."[12] Despite the slight increases in production of Mk V Panthers, arguably one of the most powerful if not best tanks of World War II, and Mk IV medium tanks, OB West could not overcome the quantitative advantage held by the Allies, especially the Americans, who by 1944 had fully mechanized and motorized forces capable of conducting swift advances once the breakout from the beachhead occurred.

In addition to the forces facing the Allies in the immediate area behind the beachhead, the strength of the German Seventh Army, which would be engaged throughout the Normandy campaign, and more specifically the fighting in the *bocage*, stood at 14 infantry (mobile and static) and four panzer divisions. Field Marshal von Rundstedt, as Commander-in-Chief, OB West, had under his command in France and in the Western theatre 58 divisions, of

■ *Left:* A lack of artillery in Normandy meant that the Germans put heavy reliance on mortars and this weapon: the 150mm Nebelwerfer 41 rocket launcher – nicknamed the "Moaning Minnie".

which 33 were static or reserve and capable of only limited defensive duties. The other 25 divisions included 13 infantry, two parachute, five army panzer, four SS panzer, and one independent panzer (the 21st), which at the time of the Normandy landings had been in the process of refitting with captured Russian equipment.[13] While German war production laboured in supplying the Wehrmacht on both the Eastern and Western Fronts with tanks, guns and other essential materiel, Allied bombing and the constant drain of much-needed replacement armour meant that first class armoured equipment remained a comparative rarity in divisions assigned to OB West until 1944, and even then it trickled in at an uneven pace.

German Command and Control

As already mentioned, Field Marshal von Rundstedt was the overall commander-in-chief of OB West, with both Field Marshal Rommel and Colonel-General von Dollman exercising immediate tactical direction of the forces in the field. While all of the German commanders in OB West had considerable experience in matters of operational expertise, what hampered the Wehrmacht in France were the divergent views held by von Rundstedt and Rommel in how to counter best the landings. As early as May 1943 senior army officers in the West acknowledged that an Anglo-American invasion of Europe was inevitable. While this, of course, would put an overwhelming strain on the German Army, it still presented an opportunity to turn the war in Germany's favour. Hitler certainly thought so. By the end of 1943 a new strategic idea was abroad in Berlin. If the Allied invasion could be held and then defeated within 32km (20 miles) of the French coast, the Western

Allies' war effort would be put back at least two years – time enough to turn all the Reich's resources towards the defeat of Russia. The question remained, however: how to achieve this victory?

Whereas von Rundstedt favoured a more mobile defence, Rommel remained convinced of the necessity of defeating the landing before it could

■ *Above:* A Mk VI Tiger tank of the 101st SS Heavy Tank Battalion, only one of three battalions to field the Tiger during the Normandy battles.

build up a bridgehead and push inland. The "Desert Fox", drawing on his experience of Allied materiel superiority in North Africa, also believed that because the Luftwaffe could not sweep the Allied planes from the skies over the battlefield in France, mobile operations, while more desirable were, in fact, impossible. Rommel maintained that because the German Army could not manoeuvre like the Allies, its only chance for a defensive success was to fight from prepared defensive positions. Pillboxes, entrenchments and other man-made fortifications of the Atlantic Wall, he asserted, were the only means available to the Germans in offsetting the superiority of the Allies in terms of

■ *Above:* A Tiger of the 102nd SS Heavy Tank Battalion. This unit was all but destroyed in fighting around Falaise in late August.

■ *Left:* Senior officers of the 101st SS Heavy Tank Battalion in a field conference. The tank ace Michael Wittmann is on the far left.

"mass and mobility". Ironically, it would be the natural terrain in the *bocage* that would offer the Americans the most trouble in advancing inland. In fact, combined with its superiority in arms and tactical handling of such weapons, in addition to the terrain found on the Cotentin Peninsula, the German Army was able to delay General Bradley's forces from conducting the mobile campaign called for in the original Overlord plan through its organization of the defences starting on the Normandy beaches and running back towards Carentan and St-Lô.[14]

While Rommel strengthened the defences up to 9.6km (six miles) inland from the beaches with man-made antitank and anti-personnel defences, particularly mines, he formed his reserves in what have been referred to as "resistance nests". Field Marshal Rommel argued that by "massing his troops" in fortified positions, he was at least providing them with some form of protection from the Allies' superiority in the air. He believed that given the Wehrmacht's chronic shortages in both men and materiel, a fixed defensive strategy was the only option available to the German Army in Normandy.[15] Rommel also believed that the mobile reserves held by OB West were "too far behind" the main battle front to be of any use in the attempt to halt the invasion before it amassed its strength and broke out of the beachhead. He maintained that:

"The dispositions of both combat and reserve forces should be such as to

■ *Right:* General Alfred Jodl, the chief of the Wehrmacht's operations staff in Berlin. Jodl advocated a defence in-depth in Normandy.

ensure that the minimum possible movement will be required to counter an attack at any of the most likely points, whether in the Low Countries, in the Channel area proper, in Normandy or in Brittany, and to ensure that the greater part of the enemy troops, sea and airborne, will be destroyed by our fire during their approach."[16]

Given the Wehrmacht's lack of armoured vehicles, small, light and heavy weapons, as well as sufficient manpower, Rommel believed that a defence centred around fixed fortifications offered the best and perhaps the only means of defeating the Allies once a landing occurred. As the fighting in the *bocage* country demonstrated, the field marshal wasn't too far off the mark.

Field Marshal von Rundstedt, on the other hand, maintained that a mobile vice – a flexible, mechanized defensive strategy – offered the best way to counter an Allied landing. During the months prior to the landings in Normandy, the commander-in-chief of OB West sought to motorize and upgrade the armaments in the static divisions engaged in coastal defence. In the Seventh Army area, von Rundstedt organized mobile *Kampfgruppen* or "battle groups" that contained a mixture of infantry, armour, artillery, and other mechanized vehicles among four of the infantry divisions (the 265th, 266th, 275th and 353rd) defending the Brittany coast. In case of an invasion of Normandy, von Rundstedt planned to move these battle groups into the combat zone.

As far as the available panzer divisions were concerned, at the beginning of June 1944 only one, the

21st, was in Normandy, with the 12th SS Panzer and Panzer *Lehr* some 100km (62 miles) farther inland. All other armoured units were positioned north of the River Seine to counter the expected Allied attack on the Pas-de-Calais – the shortest invasion route from Great Britain. If this situation were not bad enough, OB West did not have command of these panzer units. That resided solely with Hitler in Berlin. And while the three panzer divisions south of the River Seine would of course respond to any Allied attack in their region, further panzer reinforcements would require the Führer's personal order.

■ *Left:* The big guns of German coastal artillery dominated the Pas-de-Calais, but were fortunately in the wrong place to meet the Allied invasion in June 1944, which took place farther south.

■ *Right:* On the beach in summer 1944, these troops garrison just one of the thousands of emplacements along the Atlantic Wall. Many of these static units were poor quality *Ost* battalions from Eastern Europe.

In addition to the movement of units to Normandy in case of an invasion, German divisions that had previously been static were mobilized, though these efforts had only just begun when the invasion struck in June. Despite the Seventh Army's efforts at scraping together whatever motorized transport it could obtain into motorized corps transport companies, these efforts only began in May 1944. Field Marshal von Rundstedt's efforts to organize mechanization coincided with those of Rommel to muster every available man and place him along the coastline to meet the invasion. The "Desert Fox", in fact, ordered that units in and around St-Lô and Caen – two of the most important communications hubs in the region – be regrouped so as to facilitate their availability in the first hours of the Allied assault.

Hitler's View

As for Adolf Hitler, the Führer himself had undergone a change in thought as to the disposition of the mobile units behind the beach defence units. Colonel-General Alfred Jodl, Chief of the *Oberkommando der Wehrmacht* (OKW), Armed Forces High Command, pointed out to the Führer that with the exception of three divisions, all units were already far enough forward for their artillery to fire on the invasion beaches. Besides the danger associated with fixed fortifications, Jodl felt it necessary to preserve some defence in depth in order to resist probable airborne landings. Despite both von Rundstedt's and Jodl's strong objections, however, Rommel continued to shift the bulk of available forces to coastal defence. After a vehement protest from von Rundstedt that no more units be shifted to Rommel's positions along the coast, OKW in Berlin turned down Rommel's request to commit the bulk of the available reserve divisions to the defence of the possible invasion beaches.

Defensive Theories

Thus, the conflict between Rommel's and von Rundstedt's theories of defence was never adequately resolved in favour of one or the other, as events in Normandy eventually overcame both of them. This failure to find an amenable solution eventually led to a compromise between the two men and the solution agreed upon as regards troop deployments satisfied no one. In fact, the pool of mobile reserves had been cut down below what would be needed for an effective counterattack in mass. In short, the failure to reach a compromise between Rommel's static, coastline defence versus that of von Rundstedt's desire for a mobile defence once the landing took place, held German strategy hostage to a defensive campaign just as American strategy and operational planning would be forced to fight it out in the hedgerows of Normandy once the initial beachhead had been established. For the Germans, however, the operational and tactical doctrine it adopted in the *bocage* after D-Day was, in fact, due to the nature of the terrain there and was a re-affirmation – by default – of Rommel's static, defence-in-depth as opposed to von Rundstedt's concept of mobile operations: the *bocage,* after all, was as difficult for the panzers to traverse as it was for American armour.

As a consequence of this, German operational flexibility had been curtailed without having achieved a decisive thickening of the coastal defences or of strengthening the capabilities of the armoured and mobile forces.[17] Despite this, however, Field Marshal Rommel's operational plans for the coastline prepared the defenders and had a residual effect on the organization of the defence-in-depth in the *bocage* country west of Utah Beach in June and July.

The landings on 6 June 1944, however, changed all this, as the German Army in the West fought for its very survival against what was at first a trickle and later a flood of American combat troops into the Utah and Omaha beachheads. Nevertheless, the battle that would take place in the Norman *bocage* country had been already shaped, in part, by General Eisenhower's hopes to advance quickly inland, as well as Lieutenant-General Bradley's desire to conduct mobile operations once ashore and advance inland towards St-Lô. In fact, Bradley's failure to anticipate the logistical and tactical considerations of hedgerow country, coupled with the stiffening German defences, largely due to the initiative and fighting abilities of the enemy soldier in defensible terrain, made the next two months of fighting perhaps the most difficult of the entire Northwest European Campaign.

■ *Right:* General Omar N. Bradley. During the Normandy campaign Bradley, then a three-star general, commanded the First Army during the assault phase and the fighting in the *bocage*. He was promoted to command of the US Twelfth Army Group on 1 August, handing the First Army over to General Courtney H. Hodges.

CHAPTER II:

AMERICAN OPERATIONAL AND TACTICAL DOCTRINE

German tactics in the Normandy *bocage*. The weapons of the US infantry divisions and their tactics in defeating the German defences in the hedgerows.

The US Army divisions that began landing on 6 June 1944 soon discovered that the hedgerows would have a considerable influence on the speed with which operations would progress in *bocage* country. As all pre-D-Day plans for Overlord stressed, "special tactics should be developed for use in the hedgerows and work in small groups with infantry to good advantage."[1] In fact, the fighting here would offer advantages to both the attacking and defending infantry. Whereas armour could not be used in mass formations, it would be able to work alongside infantrymen with "good advantage".

Nonetheless, even though SHAEF knew of the terrain in the *bocage* country it paid little attention to the possible problems American infantry might face. As one historian wrote, "it appears as if the hostile nature of the hedgerows took senior American leaders by surprise."[2] In fact, only two

■ *Left:* US field artillery in action. As the US Army entered the war it put into practice a new artillery doctrine: plunging indirect fire in close support of infantry, and developed new guns such as this 105mm howitzer to achieve it.

days after the landings at Normandy, General Bradley referred to the *bocage* country as the "damnedest country I've seen". Other American commanders echoed similar views. Major-General J. Lawton "Lightning Joe" Collins, commanding general of VII Corps, remarked to Bradley that the terrain in the *bocage* country, "was as bad as anything he had encountered during the fighting he had experienced on Guadalcanal". Brigadier-General James M. Gavin, commanding general of the 82nd Airborne Division, in fact, seemed surprised as to the actual terrain in the *bocage* country in spite of the fact that prior to the Normandy landings there had been some talk about the hedgerows in France.

These views were held by junior officers as well, despite the fact that many American units trained in the various regions of the English countryside where there was some similarity in the type of terrain beyond the beachheads at Normandy that they might encounter. Captain Charles D. Folsom, who commanded a rifle company in the 329th Regiment in VII Corps' 83rd Infantry Division, commented that the hedgerows "presented a problem his unit never had before encountered", and that none of his unit's pre-D-Day training included combat scenarios in the hedgerows.[3]

Despite the fact that some Army units, such as the 116th and 175th Infantry Regiments, had been in England since October 1942, combat training for the European mainland had simply not been one of the army's priorities. Getting divisions formed and shipped overseas had been the main task, as had been the build-up of enough equipment and supplies to make a full-scale invasion possible.

Once the divisions were established in England, amphibious training for the

■ *Left:* Most photographs of German artillery in Normandy show it buried in camouflage. Allied air superiority made this essential, but it was also indicative of the high priority the Germans gave to camouflage and the expert use of defensive positions.

assault units were given priority, while the sheer scale of the US Army presence created its own obstacles. By May 1944 there were over 1.5 million US troops in England and precious little room for them to train. Live-firing exercises were a particular problem. Priority was given over to the British Army and the US assault divisions – what is more, up until early 1944 there had been a drastic shortage of M1 Garand rifles, and many of the new infantry divisions began their training in the US using the old M1903 Springfield model.

The hedgerows, which bottled up US troops as they pushed inland from the Normandy beaches, became in time the most important preoccupation of American fighting men during the next two months, and for many soldiers remained as their most vivid memory of France. As American troops discovered, each hedgerow was a potential fortress in which the Germans cut out foxholes, trenches and individual fighting pits or slit trenches. German defensive positions in the hedgerows were able to hinder the Americans from three sides as they attempted to move through the area. The Germans also made extensive use of anti-personnel mines. The dense undergrowth of the *bocage* in mid-summer was an ideal terrain in which to hide a wide variety of anti-personnel devices, including wooden "shoe" mines, and ball-bearing-filled "S" mines; there was also ample opportunity to tripwire the ubiquitous M1924 "Potato Masher" stick grenade.

As occurred throughout the months of June and July, the seizure of each individual hedgerow required not only firepower but the ability to adapt to the

■ *Left:* Luftwaffe ground troops lay their 88mm gun on target. Designed as an AA gun, the effectiveness of the "88" against armour was legendary.

tactical situation at hand, something Americans were still learning after being at war for two and half years. In fact, important as the battle for Normandy itself, the fighting in the hedgerows revealed a tactical dysfunction that combat in North Africa, Sicily and Italy had not corrected. The subsequent performance of the American soldier in the *bocage* country served as testimony to the US Army's failure to prepare adequately prior to D-Day for what lay ahead in France as the advance from the beachhead began in earnest after 6 June.

This chapter will examine the organization and operational and tactical doctrine of the US soldier as he prepared to fight in the *bocage* country after D-Day.

German Defensive Doctrine

Despite the problems presented by the hedgerows, the real problem, and one that is often overlooked by historians, is the fact that the Germans had organized an effective defence-in-depth. What the Germans could not accomplish at Utah and Omaha beaches, they did so in the *bocage* country, to prevent the full deployment of American combat units and to deny the First Army the space needed to outflank the German defensive positions and thus utilize its superiority in mobility. Instead, the Germans forced the Americans to fight a war of attrition, one which favoured them due to their operational and tactical superiority.

The German positions had been organized into an effective defence-in-depth specifically designed to destroy the coordination and momentum of the attacks while fully exploiting the defensive advantages afforded by the hedgerows. This defensive line established by the Germans was made up of a series of interconnected, compartmentalized fields of fire, defended

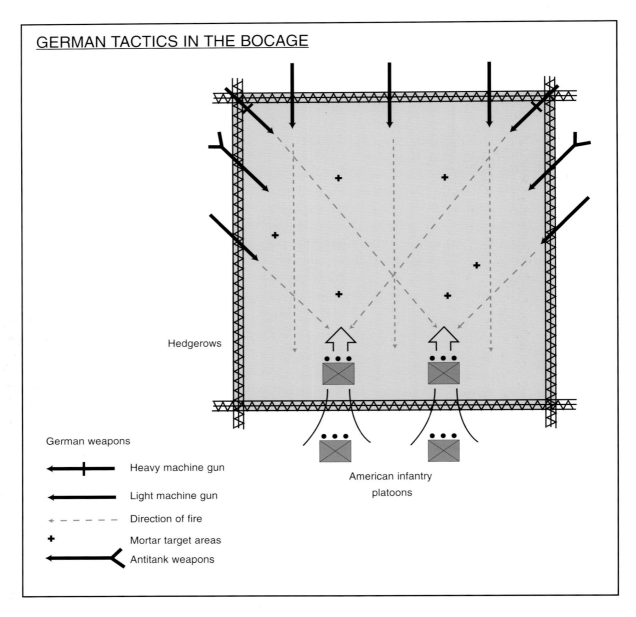

GERMAN TACTICS IN THE BOCAGE

Hedgerows

German weapons

———†——— Heavy machine gun

————— Light machine gun

– – – – – – Direction of fire

+ Mortar target areas

———< Antitank weapons

American infantry platoons

by small detachments of troops armed with a variety of small arms, light and heavy weapons. The Germans reinforced these positions with "echeloned belts" of prepared, pre-registered positions defended by artillery pieces, mostly the deadly 88mm gun, and tanks, mostly Mk V Panthers and StuG assault guns. In short, each single field inside the *bocage* became a miniature fortress, and forced the attacking American infantry to fight for each "compartment".

Much like its German counterpart, the American infantry division (Type 1944 variety) had been organized on a triangular basis. The American infantry division that landed at Normandy was based on three regiments of three battalions each. The battalions were likewise broken down into three rifle companies of three platoons each. The smallest unit inside the division was the rifle squad that consisted of 12 men armed with M1 Garand semi-automatic rifles, a Browning Automatic Rifle

■ *Right:* The result of armour on the *bocage.* A US column has ignored the sunken road (centre) and broken through the hedge banks. The small marks on the fields are German slit trenches.

■ *Above:* The problem faced by the Germans in moving their artillery on the Normandy battlefield was that it required vehicles, which meant that movements could only be safely completed at night.

(BAR), and one bolt-action M1903 Springfield sniper rifle.

The adoption of the Garand semi-automatic rifle as the US infantry's standard weapon gave the rifle platoon a powerful firepower advantage over the German infantry's bolt-action 98k Mauser. Though heavy at 4.5kg (10lb), the Garand was easier to maintain than the 1903 Springfield it replaced because it had 20 fewer working parts. It was also said to have 40 percent less recoil. Its greatest advantage in combat, however, was its rate of fire: up to 80 rounds a minute in the hands of a

trained rifleman. This meant that a 12-man rifle squad could lay down nearly a thousand rounds of .3in-calibre ammunition on a target per minute; and that was before the BAR and other support weapons came into play.

To achieve anything like this level of firepower, of course, each infantryman had to carry a lot of ammunition: 10 eight-round clips in his webbing cartridge belt and at least another six clips in a standard-issue cloth bandolier – of which some soldiers carried two. All this weight may have seemed an impediment, but not when it was a case of shooting first and

■ *Left:* A Waffen-SS crew and their 75mm AT gun command a road through the *bocage*. The priority of German guns was Allied armour.

■ *Below:* The advantage of using mortars on US infantry in the *bocage* was clear: easy camouflage; rapid fire; quick manoeuvre.

moving afterwards. And infantrymen did a lot of shooting first!

In addition to the three rifle platoons per company, there was a weapons platoon and a small headquarters section that comprised a rifle company. Each weapons platoon had two light .3in-calibre machine guns (which would be extremely useful during the fighting in the *bocage*), and the trustworthy .5in-calibre machine guns, three 60mm mortars, and three 2.36in bazooka antitank weapons. The strength of the rifle company was six officers and 187 enlisted men.[4]

US Army Infantry Squad – 1944
10 Riflemen – M1 Garand
1 Rifleman – Browning Automatic (BAR)
1 Sniper – M1903 Springfield Rifle (with grenade launcher)

Three companies, plus a heavy weapons and headquarters company, comprised a rifle battalion. The heavy weapons company came equipped with additional .3in-calibre machine guns, six 81mm mortars and seven bazookas, while the headquarters company comprised an antitank platoon of three 57mm antitank guns, three .3in-calibre and one .5in-calibre machine guns and eight bazookas. In turn, three battalions, a headquarters company, service company, antitank company, an infantry gun company (armed with 37mm weapons), and a medical detachment comprised a regiment. It was supported by six 57mm antitank guns, six 105mm howitzers and three .5in-calibre machine guns.

■ *Right:* With the huge number of Allied vehicles in Normandy it is not surprising that the Germans took advantage. Here, *Fallschirmjaeger* pose on board their captured British scout car.

While battalion-, regimental- and divisional-level commanders had at their disposal a vast array of both light and heavy infantry weapons, they nonetheless lacked the one crucial element that would prove extremely useful in the *bocage* country: the tank. Whereas the tank had been foreseen during the pre-World War II era as an infantry support and exploitation weapon, nowhere was it to be found inside the infantry division's table of organization (T/O). In order to correct this deficiency, in 1943 army planners began attaching an independent tank battalion per division known as General Headquarters (GHQ) tank units. These had the same organization as the standard US Army tank battalion of a headquarters company, a service company, three medium tank companies and a light tank company. Each tank platoon had five tanks, usually two light M-5 Stuarts and three medium M-4 76mm-armed Shermans. Every tank company had three platoons and a headquarters section of two tanks. A medium tank company had a total strength of five officers and 116 enlisted men, as well as 17 M-4 Sherman tanks. The light tank company had five officers and 91 enlisted men and came equipped with the M-5 Stuart tank.[5] GHQ tank battalions normally supported infantry divisions in the attack. In turn, a tank battalion found itself attached to one of

■ Above: Under fire, a *Fallschirm-jaeger* MG42 team race to their weapon, July 1944. The MG42 was light enough to be manned by two men, but its very high rate of fire meant that it needed a large and regular supply of ammunition.

■ *Right:* The Normandy countryside provided the perfect place for German infantry and armour to move around unseen, while the region's stone farmhouses created ideal fortifications.

■ *Right:* An impressive display of armour. The US 79th Infantry Division's tank battalion (the 749th) in the newly liberated streets of Lessay, Cotentin Peninsula, 27 July.

the division's infantry regiments in order to provide fire support to one of the battalions of that regiment.

The US Army's pre-World War II doctrine theoretically held that American infantry fought as a combined-arms team. In true combined-arms fashion, rifle battalions often went into the attack with tanks, combat engineers, artillery, service support and close air support. However, even though American rifle battalions were much better balanced, in terms of combined arms the fighting in the *bocage* country exposed just how much US infantrymen had yet to learn about the battlefield practicalities of combined arms. In fact, despite the US Army's emphasis on the combined-arms battle, as found in doctrinal publications such as FM-100-5 *Operations* (1940), whereby, "no one arm wins battles", the simple truth was that the concerted action among the combined arms remained elusive during the army's first years in World War II, due largely to its failure to learn the lessons of World War I, where the combined-arms team contributed to the Germans' battlefield defeat in 1918.[6]

Combined Arms

In the rush to field a force in 1942, army leaders failed to heed the warnings of General George C. Marshall, Army Chief-of-Staff, who at Fort Benning, Georgia, had been an advocate of combined-arms warfare during the interwar era. What failed the US Army in the early fighting in the *bocage* country was the skilful application of the combined-arms team in order to

defeat the enemy. The lessons of Kasserine Pass and of Sicily only a year earlier had to be re-learned at a frightful cost, as American troops were forced to fight for each hedgerow. In fact, whereas a German infantry company at full strength was roughly 140 men, the American rifle company had 47 more rifles at its disposal, and thus conceivably had more firepower. While organizationally the American rifle company remained dominant on the battlefield due to its overwhelming advantage in logistical and aviation assets, the German infantryman was

able to overcome his materiel shortages through operational manoeuvre and excellent tactical performance when fighting from prepared defensive positions in hedgerow terrain.

Doctrinally, the US Army had emphasized the offensive. This included overcoming enemy defences through envelopment and penetration. As for envelopments, infantry were to attack simultaneously an enemy's rear and flanks while other friendly forces attacked with the objective of seizing the enemy's rear areas. Penetrations, on the other hand, were characterized by

■ *Above:* The M1 Garand semi-automatic rifle on the Normandy frontline. The soldier third from right carries an extra six-clip bandolier. In expert hands the Garand was capable of over 80 rounds per minute.

■ *Below:* The M1903 Springfield bolt-action rifle. This was the standard US infantry weapon in 1917, but was replaced after 1936 by the M1 Garand. The M1903 continued to be used in basic training, and as a company sniper rifle.

headlong frontal assaults "designed to rupture the enemy's defensive positions" in order that the main attacking forces could maintain the offensive in order to seize and penetrate the enemy's rear areas. Because they favoured the use of fire and manoeuvre, US Army leaders emphasized fire and manoeuvre throughout infantry training, both in the United States and prior to the invasion in England. The maxim for US infantry in the attack was to "maintain the momentum" as this tended to reduce casualties, and enabled the maximum use of available firepower.

Due also to the fact that the infantry battalion was the primary manoeuvre element in the US Army, both the rifle company and platoon inside the

battalion were paramount in achieving battlefield objectives. Basic army infantry doctrine maintained that battalions achieved their objective by "fire and manoeuvre". While the battalion's light and heavy support weapons neutralized enemy defensive positions, the infantry manoeuvred against the enemy and closed in on the defender in a series of assaults whereby the individual soldier was able to employ his rifle, hand grenades and bayonet to kill or capture the defender.

Whereas the US Army's doctrinal manuals stressed fire and manoeuvre from battalions on down, most battalion-sized attacks resembled frontal assaults whereby battalions would attack along a frontage from 457m to 914m

(500 to 1000 yards) in width (depending on the terrain) with two companies abreast and one in reserve. While one of the attacking companies pressed the attack forward, the other one provided fire support with a secondary attack and fire suppression. When employing conventional tactics, rifle companies normally operated on a frontage of 182m to 417m (200 to 500 yards) wide during an attack. Historian Michael Doubler wrote that:

"During the early battles in Normandy American commanders attempted to use conventional methods of attack to root out the Germans. Infantry Companies attacked with two rifle platoons abreast followed in turn by the third rifle platoon and the weapons platoon. Because German defensive fires covered all natural breaks in the hedgerows, the lead elements were forced to make their own passageways through the dense vegetation. As the attackers emerged from the hedgerows, they found themselves exposed to almost point-blank German machine-gun fire. The Americans returned fire with their own rifles and automatic weapons, but this firepower was not enough to suppress the German defenders."[7]

Even with tanks the Americans found the going slow in hedgerow country. Tanks that operated with the infantry had as their main mission the destruction or suppression of the enemy and to keep the momentum of the attack going. While infantry was vulnerable to automatic rifle fire, tanks

■ *Right:* The first production model of the AT M1 "bazooka", 1942. This simple two-man launcher could fire a high-explosive rocket through 70mm (3in) of steel plate.

could operate with ease. Tanks, however, were very vulnerable to antitank guns and antitank mines, a point not missed by the Germans who had, by 1944, been able to overcome the Americans' numerical advantage in armoured fighting vehicles with the adoption of the *Panzerfaust*, a recoilless one-shot antitank weapon, and greater use of antitank mines.

Both the tanks and infantry, however, soon forged a very strong working relationship, one that was dependent on each other's ability to suppress enemy fire and positions during an attack. When tanks and infantry operated together, tanks normally "neutralized" or destroyed enemy automatic weapons and infantry while the infantry destroyed antitank minefields or suppressed antitank weapons such as the panzerfaust. Friendly infantry likewise protected tankers from enemy sappers that attempted to destroy the tank with hand grenades or satchel charges of TNT.

Infantry and Armour Assaults

In the attack, infantry and armour operated in two echelons with each one taking its turn in leading attacks. Armour normally led the way when the terrain was flat or rolling, with an absence of antitank obstacles. Infantry, on the other hand, normally led the attack over difficult terrain or when strong enemy minefields were present. This latter tactic was precisely how attacks in the *bocage* country were carried out. When armour led the way, the first attacking echelon was composed solely of tanks while the second echelon was a mixture of tanks and infantry. While tanks used fire and manoeuvre in order to seize their objective the infantry followed close behind. As the infantry advanced with the second echelon, the tanks provided suppressive cover fire. As the attack developed, the tanks and infantry would, in effect, "leap frog" from position to position. The same was true in the case of infantry leading the attack, though in this instance the attacking infantry in the first wave were accompanied by artillery fire. Regardless of whether tanks or infantry led the attack, American tactics soon evolved to the point that both forged an extremely effective team in seizing and clearing enemy forces from an objective.

A platoon commander's detailed description of hedgerow fighting, however, best summarizes the attitude of American combat troops as they continued to fight through what appeared to be a never-ending maze of hedgerows filled with German defenders armed with machine guns and automatic weapons:

"There were just three ways that our infantry could get through the hedgerow country. They could walk down the road, which always makes the leading men feel practically naked (and they are). They could attempt to get through gaps in the corners of the hedgerows and crawl up along the row leading forward or rush through in a group and spread out in the field beyond. This was not a popular method. In the first place often there were no gaps just when you wanted one most, and in the second place the Germans knew about them before we did and were usually prepared with machine gun and machine pistol reception committees. The third method was to rush a skirmish line over a hedgerow and then across the field. This could have been a fair method if there had been no hedgerows.

"Usually we could not get through the hedge without hacking a way through. This of course took time, and a

Right: A bangalore torpedo being prepared during training. The "torpedo" was little more than a scaffold pipe filled with high explosive, but it proved invaluable in clearing barbed wire, and later in blasting holes through the Normandy hedgerows.

German machine gun can fire a lot of rounds in a very short time. Sometimes the hedges themselves were not thick. But it still took time for the infantrymen to climb up the bank and scramble over, during which time he was a luscious target, and when he got over the Germans knew exactly where he was. All in all it was very discouraging to the men who had to go first. The farther to the rear one got the easier it all seemed.... Of course the Germans did not defend every hedgerow, but no one knew without stepping out into the spotlight which ones he did defend.

"It was difficult to gain fire superiority when it was most needed. In the first place machine guns were almost useless in the attack because about the only way they could be used was to fire from the hip. If you set them up before the advance started, they had no field of fire and they could not shoot the enemy. If you carried them along until you met the enemy, still the only way to get them in position was to set them up on top of a hedgerow bank. That was not good because the German was in the next bank and got you before you set the gun down. Anyway, it had to be laid on the bank, no tripod, just a gun barrel lying unevenly on its stomach. On the other hand, the Germans could dig their guns into the banks of the advance, camouflage them, and be all set to cover the roads, trail, and other bottlenecks our men had to use.

"The artillery was the major fire support weapon. But it suffered certain handicaps. In the first place it had to be adjusted from the frontline by forward observers. These sometimes had difficulty knowing just where they were,

■ *Left:* **US Army Rangers, who later would be one of the units to spearhead the D-Day landings, train with the Browning Automatic Rifle in Scotland in 1943.**

■ *Left:* The M-5 Stuart tank. By 1944 the Stuart was nearly obsolete, but still did useful service in a reconnaissance role

■ *Below:* The US Army's main company support weapon was the M1919 Browning light machine gun, here in its other role on an M-5 Stuart tank.

and the trees frequently delayed adjustment because of the short vision. If you found the enemy in the next hedgerow he was frequently less than 100 yards from you, and that was too close for artillery fire, particularly since short rounds would probably burst in the trees over your men in your own hedgerow. If the enemy was two or more hedgerows ahead of you, that wasn't so good either, because the mere delay in getting him through that last hedgerow just in front of him gave him time to rise up and smite you after the artillery had lifted. The mortars were effective providing you knew just what to shoot at and where it was, but the infantrymen still had the delay and exposure of getting through the last hedgerow. The Germans, being on

the defensive, profited by these minor items on the terrain. They could dig in, site their weapons to cover the approaches, and prepare tunnels and other covered exits for themselves. Then when our men appeared, laboriously working their way forward, the Germans could knock off the first one or two, cause the others to duck down behind the bank, and then call for their own mortar support. The German mortars were very, very efficient. By the time our men were ready to go after him, the German and his men and guns had obligingly retired to the next stop. If our men had rushed him instead of ducking down behind the bank, his machine gun or machine pistol would knock a number off. For our

infantrymen, it was what you might call in baseball parlance, a fielder's choice. No man was very enthusiastic about it. But back in the dugout I have often heard the remark in tones of contempt and anger, 'Why don't they get up and go?'

"The tanks are no better off. They have two choices. They can go down the roads, which in this case were just mud lanes, often too narrow for a tank, often sunk four to six feet below the adjacent banks, and generally deep in mud. The Class 4 roads were decent in spots, but only for one-way traffic, with few exits to the adjacent fields. An armoured outfit, whether it is a platoon or an armoured army, attacking along a single road attacks on a front of one tank. The rest of the tanks are just roadblocks trailing along behind. When the first tank runs into a mine or an 88 or 75 shell, it always stops, and it usually burns up. And it efficiently blocks the road so the majestic column of roaring tanks comes to an ignominious stop. The next step is to try to find out where the enemy gun or tank is, and wheel up a tank or to shoot at him. The only trouble is, that probably only the men in the first tank saw his gun flash, and they aren't talking anymore. The tanks trying to get into position to do some shooting are easily seen and get shot before they can do much about it. I have seen it happen. In the hedgerows it is almost impossible to get firing positions in the front row, and in the rear you can't see the enemy anyway so no one bothers. Usually the tanks waited for the infantry to do something about it . . .

"Instead of charging valiantly down the road, the tanks may try to bull their way through the hedgerows. This is very slow and gives the enemy time to get his tanks or guns where they can do the most good. Then he just waits. And in the solution, there is always a minor and local problem to be solved, a problem

which caused a certain amount of irritation, and that is, who is going over the hedgerow first, the infantry or the tank? It is surprising how self-effacing most men can be in such situations.

"Anyone who actually fought in the hedgerows realizes that at best the going was necessarily slow, and that a skilful, defending force could cause great delay and heavy losses to an attacking force many times stronger. This is because the attacker can't use his firepower effectively and because he can't advance rapidly except on the road where he is quickly stopped at some convenient spot.

"There were a number of other factors which contributed to the difficulties of fighting through the hedgerows. The area was merely a succession of small enclosed pastures with a few orchards, likewise enclosed by hedgerows. Seldom could one see clearly beyond the confine of the field. It was difficult to keep physical contact with adjacent squads, platoons, or larger units. It was difficult to determine exactly where one was. Unlike conditions in open country, flanks could not be protected by fields of fire. All of these contributed to the difficulties of control and caused a feeling of isolation on the part of small units. All this meant that the frontline troops thought their neighbours were nowhere around. They could not see them, they were not in the adjacent field, therefore they were behind. Often this feeling of being out on a limb would cause the leading elements to halt and wait for the flank units to come up (and sometimes these were ahead).... German counterattacks in the hedgerows failed largely for the

■ *Left:* By 8 June US paratroopers had gained objectives such as St-Marcouf behind Utah Beach. But they would not be secure until the arrival of seaborne forces.

same reasons our own advance was slowed. Any attack quickly loses its momentum, and then because of our artillery and fighter-bombers the Germans would suffer disastrous loss. In fact, we found that generally the best way to beat the Germans was to get them to counterattack – provided we had prepared to meet them."[8]

In keeping with the use of combined arms in both fire and manoeuvre against enemy positions, army doctrine also stressed the use of field artillery in both a direct and indirect manner. The artillery's role in the combined-arms attack was the neutralization of enemy machine guns and mortars, destruction of fixed enemy defensive positions, and the prevention of the enemy's ability to maintain their defensive positions as the attack against them progressed. Also used in this combined-arms attack, and especially against fixed fortifications or positions, were combat engineers. Engineers planted demolitions to destroy either enemy positions or hinder his ability to retreat or attack. Complementing the combined-arms team was the use of close air support. In the *bocage* country, as elsewhere, commanders often found it difficult if not impossible to employ effectively close air support due to technical as well as doctrinal problems, problems that had not been resolved since the beginning of the war regarding the integration of effective close air support.

Doctrinally, the fighting in the *bocage* country tested American commanders from second lieutenants to major-generals as they attempted to find a solution to affect a breakthrough. Due

to the stress placed on "fire and manoeuvre" in prewar manuals and training, as well as the limited manoeuvre room afforded by the hedgerows themselves, American commanders were forced to advance through *bocage* country "head first" and to conduct bloody frontal assaults against well-prepared German defences in terrain that favoured the defender more than the attacker. Fighting in *bocage* country tested the individual fighting abilities of not only the German but also the American soldier's ability to overcome what both man and nature had conceived as an almost impenetrable series of natural fortresses. In the end, it was left to the individual soldier and his ability to innovate in the face of combat.

While the army's prewar doctrine could not have foreseen the difficulties that American troops would face in the *bocage* country, American commanders had overestimated their own pre-D-Day planning and underestimated the ability of the Germans to prepare an adequate defensive line to block the American advance towards Carentan and St-Lô. Furthermore, as a recent scholarship on the D-Day campaign now suggests, the criticism launched against Field Marshal Sir Bernard L. Montgomery and his handling of the Twenty-First Army Group: namely his methodical approach to pre-battle preparation, has been both unfair and unwarranted. In fact, it is quite conceivable that had Lieutenant-General Bradley used Field Marshal Montgomery's pre-battle preparations before attacking the hedgerows more American lives would have been spared, and the German defences could have been cracked sooner. Instead, what followed was a bloody war of attrition that resembled the battles of World War I and not the operations envisaged by the Overlord planners.[7]

CHAPTER III:

"THE FIGHT FOR THE HEDGEROWS" PHASE ONE

The advance inland as German defences stiffen. The first moves towards St-Lô. The capture of Cherbourg.

E ven before US troops advanced beyond the beachhead, US paratroopers began to encounter what would become a two-month ordeal of fighting among the hedgerows. In fact, before dawn on D-Day, paratroopers of the 82nd and 101st Airborne Divisions had already been fighting amongst the hedgerows as they seized their assault objectives. Colonel Robert F. Sink, commanding officer of the 506th Parachute Infantry Regiment, had the mission of capturing the area near the western edge of Audonville-la-Hubert and Pouppeville, as well as the two bridges at le Port, in order to secure a passage for ground units advancing inland from the beachhead. Like many other US airborne and glider units that night, the paratroopers of the 506th became separated from each other during the drop. Colonel Sink's force set out to organize some semblance of resistance and establish strongpoints behind Utah Beach on the Cotentin

■ *Left:* A German mine buried in a hedgerow has just exploded, killing a member of a US patrol. This could herald the start of a German attack or just be another reminder of how arbitrary the killing in the *bocage* could be.

Peninsula. As would be the case throughout the fighting in the *bocage*, Colonel Sink spent most of the time attempting to re-establish contact with his other units as the hedgerows proved as formidable as the German Army, which by this time was recovering from the initial shock of the invasion. As Colonel Sink's paratroops experienced on the night of 5/6 June, the marshy terrain, coupled with the thick hedgerows, channelled their advance forward as the German infantry pinned them down with rifle, machine-gun and mortar fire. This situation repeated itself time and again across the breadth of the landing areas as American troops began pushing out from their lodgement at Omaha and Utah beaches, only to have the attack halted by stiff German resistance coming from the hedgerows.

Initial Contact

In fact, across the neck of Cotentin Peninsula the hedgerows formed a natural line of defence more formidable than the Germans themselves could have constructed. Nonetheless, General Bradley, and the other American commanders, had hoped not only to annihilate the German divisions that lay in their path but to achieve a major breakthrough into the interior of France. Unfortunately for the Americans, the *bocage* country forced them to fight the Normandy campaign on the Wehrmacht's terms, since the latter could neither be outflanked nor enveloped as called for in American operational and tactical doctrine.

The first American unit to experience the frustration of fighting the Germans in the hedgerow or *bocage* country was the 38th Infantry Regiment, which had been assigned the task of seizing Trévières. Held up by a stubborn German force and lacking a sufficient number of mortars and

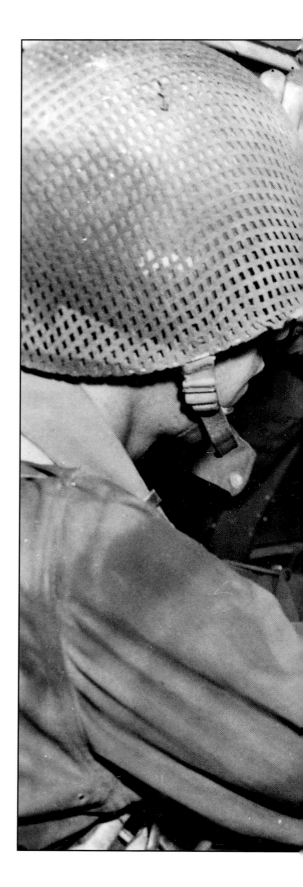

■ *Right:* Paratroopers hooked to the aircraft's static line prepare to jump. Over 13,000 US airborne troops were earmarked for Overlord. Planners reckoned their casualty rate would be nearly 50 percent.

machine guns, the fighting that took place in the hedgerows was painfully slow. The River Aure had been selected as the line of departure for the regiment but, both its 2nd and 3rd Battalions ran into heavy German fire before reaching it. Progress was slow. As they tried to advance, soldiers were continually pinned down by German machine guns that proved too difficult to locate among the hedgerows, and still more difficult to neutralize with only light infantry weapons. While the soldiers of the 38th Infantry Regiment were given direct support by accurate artillery fire provided by the 38th Field Artillery Battalion, the Germans refused to give

■ *Left:* Landing 8km (five miles) from their DZ, men of the 82nd Airborne skirt the church at St-Marcouf on their way back to the division.

■ *Above:* By 8 June forces from Utah had pushed up to 3 km (two miles) inland, though the flooded terrain and the *bocage* were beginning to slow the advance.

ground. Finally, however, the 3rd Battalion was able to move across the Aure under heavy German machine-gun fire due mainly to the efforts of Captain Omery C. Weathers, Company K's commanding officer, who led his men through the hail of German machine-gun fire at the cost of his own life. For his bravery and leadership under fire, Captain Weathers was posthumously awarded the Distinguished Service Cross. The 38th Regiment's commanding officer, Colonel Walter A. Elliott, also exhibited intrepidity under fire as he went among the various battalions pushing and urging them forward. By midnight of 9/10 June, the

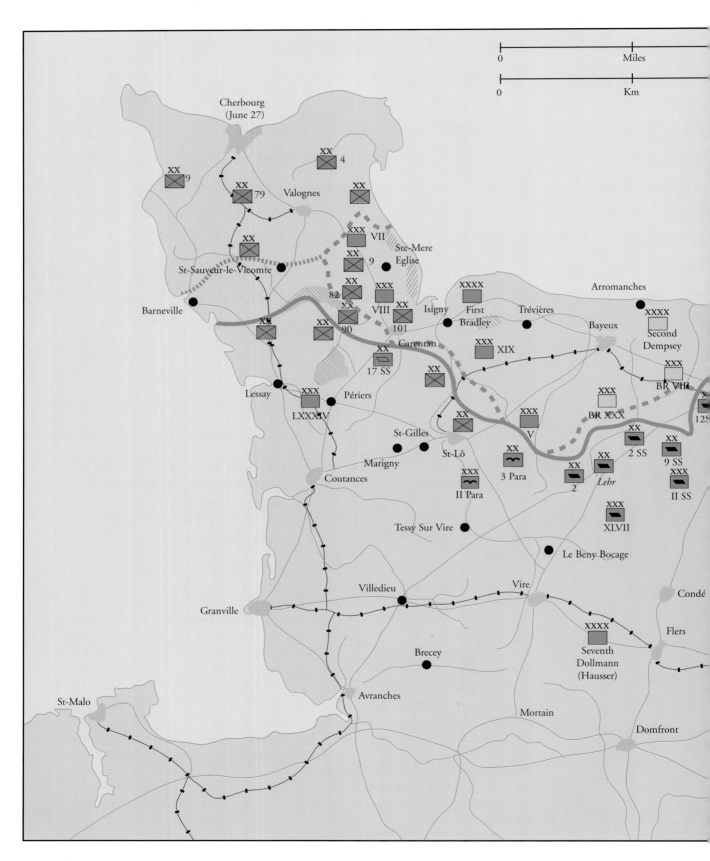

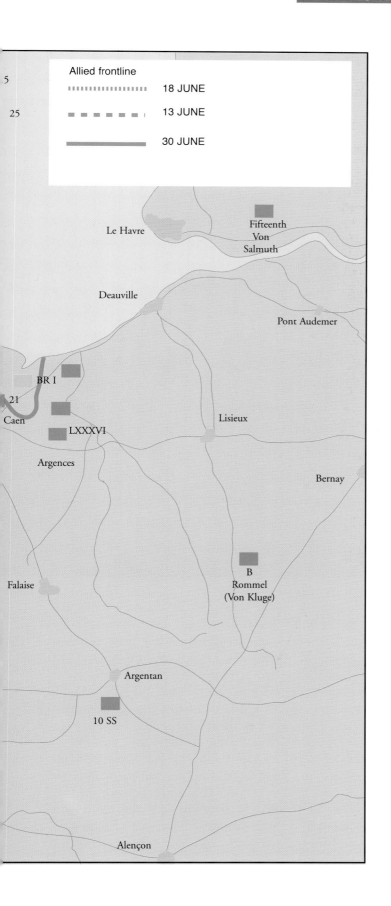

Allied frontline

.... 18 JUNE

▬ ▬ ▬ ▬ ▬ ▬ 13 JUNE

▬▬▬▬▬▬ 30 JUNE

2nd Battalion, with the exception of a small edge of a strongpoint on the southern edge of town, had occupied Trévières, which the soldiers "mopped up" the following morning.

The 1st Battalion, 38th Infantry, was also forced to fight it out with the remnants of the German 352nd Division which had dug itself in at the Haute-Littee crossroads near the Forêt de Cerisy in the so-called Caumont Gap. Here, the infantrymen of the 1st Battalion eventually overcame the light German resistance and artillery that bombarded their positions as the enemy withdrew. Even as the German 352nd and 716th Divisions withdrew, the Panzer *Lehr* Division continued attacking at Longraye. The 38th Infantry was, however, able to advance through the gap that had been opened up to Caumont. Meanwhile Colonel-General Dollman ordered the bulk of the 3rd Parachute Division, as well as the 37th SS Panzergrenadier Regiment east of Avranches, while the bulk of the 17th SS Panzergrenadier Division was sent southwest of Carentan.

For the next two weeks, the US 1st Infantry Division, "Big Red One", fought it out with elements of Panzer *Lehr* and the 3rd Parachute Division, while other V Corps units mounted a series of attacks designed to assist the British 7th Armoured Division (part of the British Second Army) in its attempt to outflank Caen. The 1st Division's objective was to capture the high ground at Caumont. In order to prevent a breakthrough of its lines by Panzer *Lehr*, Major-General Clarence R. Huebner, commanding general of the 1st Division, ordered strict control over the attack. Constrained by the hedgerows, the regiments of the division

■ *Left:* **The situation in Normandy between 13 and 30 June 1944.**

■ *Above:* A tracked US 155mm gun bombards German positions south of the town of Bayeux. This unit would have come ashore on Omaha Beach. The large white star on the barrel is to avoid any danger of "friendly fire" from aircraft.

were to move over the terrain in "bounds" and be prepared to defend successive phase lines.

The attacks on either side of the army boundary lines at first seemed to promise rapid and spectacular success. The 1st Division, which jumped off at 08:00 hours with the 18th and 26th Infantry Regiments on a 2743m (3000-yard) frontage, behind a screen of two troops of the 102nd Cavalry Squadron, moved rapidly against the light enemy forces it came up against. The 18th Infantry had reached the Caumont-St-Lô highway by evening and sent patrols

into Caumont. At the same time, the 26th Infantry got one battalion to the edge of Caumont but then ran into determined resistance from an estimated two companies of Germans who belonged to the 2nd Panzer Division's reconnaissance battalion. The Germans put up a stiff fight and the town was not cleared until the following morning.

Meanwhile, the 2nd Panzer Division had launched a series of fierce counter-attacks designed to break apart the two British divisions (7th Armoured and 50th Infantry) between Cahanges and Villers-Bocage. The fighting raged for the next week as two regiments of the US 2nd Division and the entire 29th Division ran into a series of prepared defence-in-depth positions, as well as small counterthrusts aimed at the flanks of the American forces mounted by the men of the 3rd Parachute Division, who were "some of the best and toughest infantrymen in Rundstedt's armies."[1]

On 13 June, the 2nd Division renewed its attack along with the 38th Infantry, and with heavy artillery support advanced about 3.2km (two miles) south of the Elle. Enemy resistance, however, stiffened as the American troops were finally halted on orders from division headquarters on 15 June after having gained only a few kilometres. In the two-day offensive, the

2nd Division suffered 540 killed in action, most of them in the two regiments that had attempted to dislodge the Germans from Hill 192.

Meanwhile, the 29th Division had launched an attack on 12 June with one regiment, the 115th, while the 175th Infantry held ground north of the Elle protecting the corps' west flank. The 116th remained in corps reserve. As was the case in the *bocage*, the 115th, even with the direct support of three battalions of artillery, had a "hard going" as the defending Germans stopped the attack dead in its tracks with small-arms fire. The 3rd Battalion succeeded in crossing the river and advanced about 2743m (3000 yards) before enemy forces positioned inside

■ *Below:* An M-5 Stuart tank finds the enemy. The thin armour of the Stuart has been bolstered by the crew with spare track on the turret and sandbags over the front hull. Hardly the actions of a confident crew!

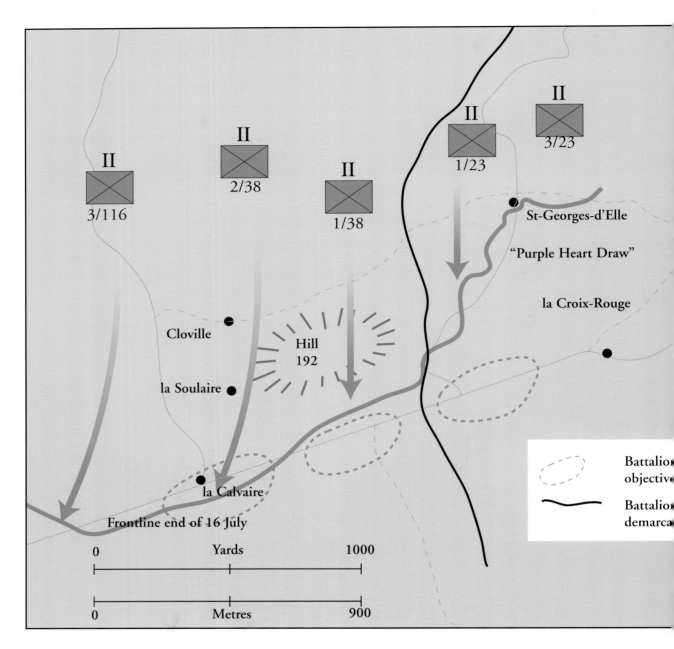

II
3/116

II
2/38

II
1/38

II
1/23

II
3/23

St-Georges-d'Elle

"Purple Heart Draw"

la Croix-Rouge

Cloville

Hill
192

la Soulaire

la Calvaire

Frontline end of 16 July

0	Yards	1000

0	Metres	900

Battalion
objective

Battalion
demarcation

the hedgerows stopped the attack (the Americans halted in fear of being cut off and annihilated). In the advance, the 115th attacked with two battalions abreast after 20 minutes of intense shelling by four artillery battalions. After crossing the stream, Company I and a platoon of Company K managed to reach the point east of the north-south road to St-Jean-de-Savigny, while the rest of the battalion followed

shortly. German resistance then increased as the 1st Battalion was stopped at the stream by heavy and accurate small-arms fire, with some support from mortars and antitank guns. This situation left the 3rd Battalion advancing with open flanks south of St-Jean-de-Savigny, where it too was stopped by machine-gun fire from hedgerow positions that could not be found. Just then a German

■ *Above:* The attack of the 2nd and 3rd Battalions, 38th Infantry, through Hill 192, 11 July. In support were two battalions of the 23rd Infantry and the 3rd Battalion of the 116th Infantry.

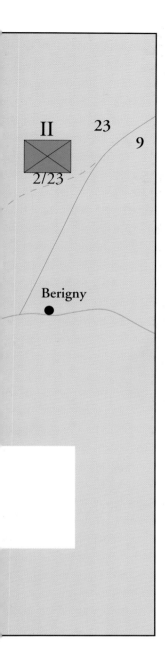

motorized column, along with some armoured vehicles, appeared north of the road to Couvains and deployed in the hedgerows to the east and west. By the end of the morning the 3rd Battalion was fighting on the defensive to avoid being cut off from the rest of the division. The intensity of the fighting resulted in the soldiers of the 3rd Battalion running precariously low on ammunition; while to make matters worse the majority were being pinned down by accurate enemy mortar and close-range shelling from antitank and self-propelled guns. In the early afternoon, such was the intensity of the fighting, Companies K and I withdrew to their original starting positions. Meanwhile, those units of the 115th that had been unable to withdraw immediately due to the heavy enemy fire fought their way through the German positions and rejoined their parent units. That afternoon, two platoons of tanks supporting the infantry were forced to give up the attack when three of their number were destroyed by German troops firing panzerfausts. With the support of artillery, however, the 115th Infantry Regiment eventually seized its objective, though at a cost. In the two days of fighting for St-Calir-sur-Elle, the 29th Division suffered 547 killed, wounded and missing. The engagement at the Elle on 12–13 June was, in fact, a foretaste of the bitter fighting to come in this sector as it appeared that the Germans were determined to hold Hill 192 with every means at their disposal.

These scenes were repeated throughout the hedgerow country. In another instance, when the 120th Infantry, a regiment from the 30th Division of the newly activated XIX Corps attempted to secure the high ground between St-Georges de Bohon (4.8km – three miles – northwest of Carentan), le Hommet d'Arthenay (4.8km – three miles – northwest of Pont Hebert) and St-Lô-la Barre de Semilly, a platoon of German soldiers with supporting machine guns held the attack up nearly all day before the regiment seized Montmartinen-Graignes. In the fight that ensued, the 120th incurred 20 percent casualties. The growing strength of German resistance can be seen in the fact that after this first battle for St-Lô, when the 29th Division was only 8km (five miles) from the town, it would take nearly six weeks of further fighting before the town was finally captured on 18 July. As for the fight for Hill 192, the 2nd Division did not capture it until 11 July, and then only after fighting for every hedgerow on its slopes, such was the ferocity of the German resistance.

Defences on Hill 192

In fact, the Germans made good use of well-prepared defensive positions on Hill 192. Here, as well as elsewhere in the Cotentin Peninsula and around Carentan, the Germans had employed mobile tactics, involving infiltration and local counterattacks to disrupt the US advance on its flanks, which were normally weak as the Americans pressed the centre in the attack. These were the very same tactics that Field Marshal von Rundstedt had advocated before the invasion, and had thus far created a formidable defence that the American soldiers had found difficult to overcome. In fact, elements of several German units, mostly armour from the 17th SS Panzergrenadier Division, 30th Mobile Brigade, and infantry from the 352nd Division, had rallied after their earlier reverses and were now putting up a determined fight. North of St-Claire-sur-Elle, the Germans had made maximum use of prepared positions. Also, by 10 June, the 3rd Parachute

■ *Left:* An essential part of the infantry heavy weapons company was the 81mm mortar. Trackways between hedgerows created excellent mortar pits. The tubes bottom right held the mortar bombs.

Division started to arrive in the Normandy area and began to make its presence known to the American troops, who noticed a marked qualitative increase in the fighting abilities of the German soldiers they now faced.

As the month of June wore on and American forces fought their way through the hedgerows, German resistance continued to stiffen with gains being measured in yards per day, not miles. The US 2nd Division, for example, in an attack launched on 16 June 1944 which began for all three regiments at 08:00 hours, had managed to push both flanks forward but was unable to advance in the centre. All along the line the enemy put up a skilful and stubborn defence in positions that made maximum use of the tangled hedgerow country. The experience of one platoon of the 9th Infantry Regiment on the left flank was typical of the fighting in the *bocage*. The platoon, advancing through open fields, was hit by fire from eight machine guns emplaced in the network of hedgerows; its leader was killed as well as a third of its men. Through its command and observation from the high ground west of St-Germain-d'Elle, the enemy repeatedly permitted the attackers to reach exposed positions which they then covered with withering small-arms and machine-gun fire. At the end of the day the 9th Infantry had lost 140 men, with 20 of them killed in the assault, and had been able to advanced only a few hundred yards.

There were some successes, however, as the most important advance that day occurred on the 2nd Division's right flank, where the 3rd Battalion, 38th Infantry, pushed up Hill 192 to within 640m (700 yards) of the crest. The value of this success, however, was limited by the failure of units on the right and left flanks to keep up with each other. The

23rd Infantry in the centre of the division's zone fought hard all day, losing 11 officers and 162 men. The end of the day found the 23rd Infantry still virtually at the line of departure. Despite the exposed position of the battalion on Hill 192, it was decided to leave it in place, as well as reinforce it with the 2nd Engineer Battalion, whose men fought as riflemen. Despite this renewed attack against Hill 192, the Germans stubbornly held on as the 2nd Division, on V Corps' order, went on to the defensive.

Meanwhile, the 29th Division opened an attack against the German-held positions atop the plateau between Bois du Bretel and la Blotrie with elements of the 1st and 3rd Battalions of the 116th Infantry, commanded by Colonel Charles D. Canham, attacking in "bounds" or leaps in order to neutralize the hedgerows. After seizing this objective, the battalions reorganized and prepared to launch attacks against Hills 147 and 150 on the Martinville Ridge. The 3rd Battalion, 115th

■ *Above:* From their uniforms, these men are former armoured vehicle crew. The destruction of whole German armoured divisions left little for these men to do but try and escape east.

Infantry, attached to the 29th Division for this operation, was to advance southwest to cut the St-Lô-Isigny highway near la Fossardiere and organize the high ground there for an all-around defence. The 2nd Battalion, 116th Infantry, then in contact with German forces dug in around St-Claire-d'Elle, were to then break contact and re-assemble in the vicinity of Couvains and be prepared to strike through the other two battalions to take Hill 115 and the stretch of highway near la Luzerne.

The two battalions that led the attack (Colonel Canham's 1st and the 3rd of the 115th) each had eight tanks attached for support. The attack order emphasized the preparation of all captured objectives for defence against expected enemy counterattacks. The 115th Infantry, less its 3rd Battalion, was held in corps reserve near the village of Ste-Marguerite-d'Elle.

Initially, the attack commenced on time and by 09:30 hours that morning the lead battalions had reported good progress against what commanders described as minimal opposition. About noon, however, the 3rd Battalion, 115th Infantry, reported meeting two German infantry companies along with two tanks. By mid-afternoon, after a furious battle, two of the 115th's supporting tanks had been knocked out with forward progress at a standstill east of les Foulons. At the same time, the 1st Battalion, 116th Infantry, was far to the south, only about 914m (1000 yards) short of St-André-de-l'Epine. Here, it was stopped by a determined German counterattack that included a massive artillery barrage. The 2nd Battalion, committed about noon to attack towards la Luzerne, was held up just west of the highway near Villiers-Fossard where the enemy was dug in on

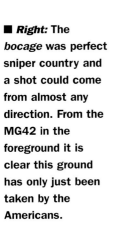

■ *Right:* The *bocage* was perfect sniper country and a shot could come from almost any direction. From the MG42 in the foreground it is clear this ground has only just been taken by the Americans.

85

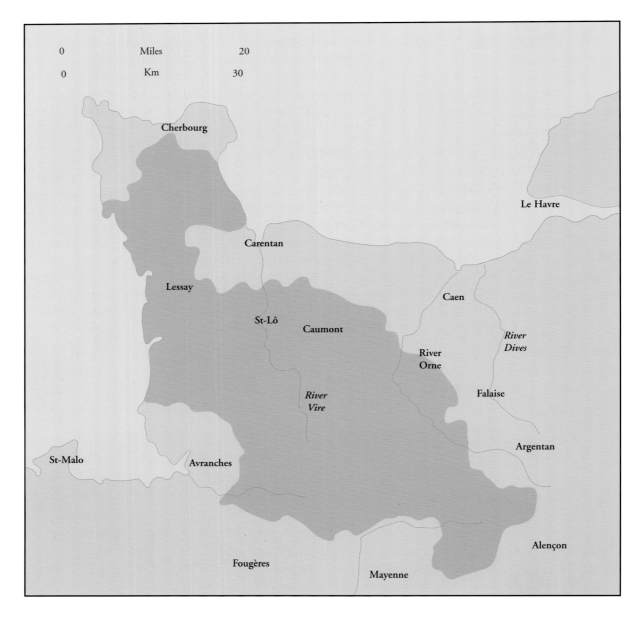

0 Miles 20

0 Km 30

a nose of high ground. Supporting artillery fire failed to shake the battalion loose. The 3rd Battalion, 115th Infantry, in the meantime, was withdrawn 914m (1000 yards) to the rear. By 18:00 hours, Major-General Charles H. Corlett, XIX Corps' commander, had called off the attack and ordered all battalions to dig in and hold for the night and resume the attack the following day.

While enemy resistance from the commanding high ground and the hedgerows had been stubborn, Colonel Canham was nevertheless not satisfied with the effort his regiment had made. In fact, he urged his subordinate commanders on that night to take up the attack the next day with increased energy.[2] Colonel Canham specifically told them that "they should advance their units on a broad front . . . and get around the sniper and machine gunner and wipe him out.... If you allow your unit to bunch up behind a hedgerow and wait for hours you are only playing

■ *Above:* **The extent of the Normandy *bocage* in 1944. Given the sheer size of the area, it is amazing that the invasion planners did not realize that the First Army's divisions might have difficulties traversing it.**

into Jerry's hand. He will move around where he can enfilade you or drop artillery or mortar fire on you... It is time to get over the jitters and fight like hell."[3]

The 175th Infantry, commanded by Lieutenant-Colonel Alexander George, met much lighter resistance as it attacked with its right flank along the River Vire. The 1st and 3rd Battalions, north of the River Elle, were relieved during the night of 15/16 June by elements of the 119th Infantry, and crossed the river to gain a line of departure along the ridge line on its south bank. While this move was made with little opposition, the battalion ran into heavy rifle, mortar, machine-gun and artillery fire as it pushed south to reach the towns of Amy and les Buteaux. The rapid advance of the 175th Infantry led General Corlett to believe mistakenly that the enemy opposition in the zone had cracked. What this advance meant, in fact, was that the battle had reached a stalemate.

Attack on Villiers-Fossard

On 17 June the 116th Regiment renewed the attack at 04:00 hours and ran into heavy German machine-gun and mortar fire. The worst spot was in the gap of about 914m (1000 yards) which had developed due to the 175th's rapid advance. There, in the vicinity of Villiers-Fossard, the enemy was strongly entrenched. Major-General Charles H. Gerhardt, the commanding officer of the 29th Division, recalled that this area was, "a devil of a place. Every time they go forward they are driven back." Unable to bring its 4.2in mortars into play against the entrenched Germans due to the poor fields of fire and observation amongst the hedgerows, the enemy positions had to be destroyed one at a time. While sources of this German fire could be located it could seldom be pinpointed as the enemy were

able to withdraw from their positions largely undetected.

This was true throughout the *bocage*. Even artillery proved ineffective, as the Germans thinly garrisoned their forward positions until after the inevitable American artillery preparatory fires which signalled an attack. Then the Germans could rapidly reinforce these well-concealed positions and meet the advancing infantry. This happened to the 115th Infantry in an attack launched on 17 June at 18:40 hours, when, after losing its direction by wandering into an orchard surrounded by a massive hedgerow, the Germans opened up with heavy machine-gun fire with the inevitable withdrawal to the original line of departure.

German Losses

Yet the Germans had also suffered in this battle of attrition. After two days of attacks the German 352nd Division had incurred some 500 casualties and had been reduced to a regimental-sized battle group. The 352nd was reinforced, however, by Battle Group *Boehm* of the 353rd Division, which had arrived in the sector from Brittany. Colonel Boehm, who was commander of the 943rd Regiment, brought up two infantry battalions and a few supporting troops on bicycles, and positioned his force into the area of le Luzerne. Colonel Boehm's troops fought hard in the Villiers-Fossard salient throughout the 17th. There were further positive developments for the Germans elsewhere, as the 3rd Parachute Battalion took up positions and entrenched itself into the battle line.

In the 175th Infantry's sector, only the 1st Battalion attacked. On Hill 108 the Americans ran into heavy German artillery fire and radioed back to headquarters that they could no longer sustain the advance. Meanwhile, the 2nd Battalion reported an enemy counterattack that appeared to be aimed at cutting off the 1st Battalion. While the Germans were able to penetrate the American lines, the attack southwards by the 175th was effectively halted.

On 18 June, the third day of the 29th Division's offensive, an eight-battalion artillery barrage failed to dislodge the German defenders who then opened up on the advancing 115th Infantry with mortar, machine-gun and artillery fire. In fact, the Germans turned the attack sectors into a "hornet's nest", and effectively blocked the advance of the 115th and 116th Infantry Regiments. The toll on the regiments was exacting. The 1st Battalion commander reported that "he hardly had anyone left" to attack with. His executive officer reported that the battalion had been effectively burnt out, and that everyone was physically exhausted. There were no leaders left, and little organization.

The 175th Infantry had a similar experience. Although its 3rd Battalion attacked south towards le Carillon without meeting much opposition, this was not so for the 1st Battalion, which had been assigned the task of seizing Hill 108. Throughout 18 June, the Germans battered the 1st Battalion and impeded its progress so much that the 3rd Battalion had to be diverted to assist it in the assault.

The area occupied by units from V Corps on 18 June were held for the next two weeks. Less than 8km (five miles) from the key town of St-Lô, the 29th Division would not enter it for almost a month and only then at a cost of some of the most intense and deadly fighting

■ *Right:* This hedge on wheels is in fact a German armoured car mounting a quadruple 20mm antiaircraft gun. Allied air superiority undermined German infantry success in holding the *bocage*.

of the war. As the US Army's official history stated, the soldiers of the 29th Division had received "a foretaste of the struggle . . . [to] . . . come . . . as V Corps mired in the hedgerow country. Due to its reliance on the tank-infantry team, the Germans were able to effectively counter it through the use of well-concealed defenses in the hedges that combined antitank guns and automatic weapons. This prevented American commanders from properly coordinating assaults led by the tank-infantry teams. Tanks could not go forward to knock out the offending machine guns, nor was the infantry able to spearhead the advance and knock out the antitank guns for it exposed them to murderous enemy fire." The effect of the German defences in the hedgerows was described in an after-action report by the 747th Tank Battalion following a limited-objective

■ *Below:* The 37mm PAK antitank gun was widely used in Normandy. Being small enough to manhandle, it was ideal to manoeuvre through hedges and fields.

■ *Right:* The 7.5cm PAK 40 had a longer range, and was positioned to give a broad field of fire: in this instance across open fields towards an expected advance of Allied armour.

attack launched on 20 June in order to reduce the Villiers-Fossard salient.

"At 06:00 Company B moved forward, with the engineers blowing gaps in hedgerows and the infantry following. The infantry was pinned down and tanks could not move further forward. But they were on part of their objective. Tanks were forced to withdraw due to heavy antitank fire and bazooka fire. One tank was knocked out and the crew of five men were wounded. The tanks kept trying to move forward, but got stuck. And the infantry stayed pinned down. Another tank was hit. On order of the regimental commander four tanks forced their way through fire to the objective. No infantry followed. Two tanks returned; one was knocked out by antitank guns. The other was stuck so that [the] crew had to abandon [the] tank as no help could reach them. The infantry withdrew 900 yards [822m] and took up defensive positions. The tanks covered the withdrawal."[4]

As the units of V Corps settled in along the front and re-grouped for the renewed effort towards St-Lô, US Army commanders began to absorb the

lessons of this first round of fighting in the hedgerows. One solution they came up with was the development of the small infantry-tank teams which could advance together. To make this possible Army engineers and technicians devised hedgerow cutters that they welded onto the fronts of the Sherman tanks in order to allow them to plough through the earthen banks that had been the source of all of their trouble. While this was going on, army communications personnel tackled the problems of direct communication between the infantry and the tanks. More importantly, however, as both the Germans and Americans regrouped for the forthcoming battles that lay ahead, American infantrymen and tank crews worked day and night to perfect the tank-infantry tactics which would allow General Bradley and his subordinate commanders to resume the offensive towards St-Lô.

The only action to take place during the remaining weeks in June was a limited attack launched by Brigadier-General Leonard T. Gerow with the recently arrived 3rd Armored Division at Villiers-Fossard, in order to eliminate an enemy position along the 29th Division's lines, thereby securing a more favourable "jump off" position once the attack towards St-Lô resumed. Also, on 20 June, three divisions of Collins' VII Corps, the 4th, 79th and 9th, closed in on Cherbourg. The first attack went in on 22 June, and by the 23rd the German defences had been breached, mainly by the 9th Division driving in from the west. However, German forces retreated into fortified areas within the town and did not surrender until 1 July, by which time the port facilities – which had been a major strategic objective of the SHAEF planners – had been so badly damaged by German demolition engineers as to make them completely useless.

Action after Cherbourg

A major objective of First Army had been taken, and the Cotentin Peninsula cleared of the enemy. However, the German LXXXIV Corps still held the line from Lessay on the coast east through Périers and on to St-Lô, and into this 35km (22-mile) front was pushing six infantry divisions, three panzer divisions (including 2nd SS Panzer) and the 17th SS Panzergrenadier Division. The fighting in the *bocage* and the need to take Cherbourg had taken valuable time. The original Overlord plan had called for a breakout from the lodgement area at D+14 (20 June), it was now approaching D+30 and still the army was fighting only 16km (10 miles) from the landing beaches.

This could be put down to the combat inexperience of Bradley's infantrymen – a crisis of morale – or a lack of aggression on the part of the commander himself. Either way the buildup of American troops and materiel on the beaches was fast reaching a critical mass. Through sheer weight of men and equipment – and the

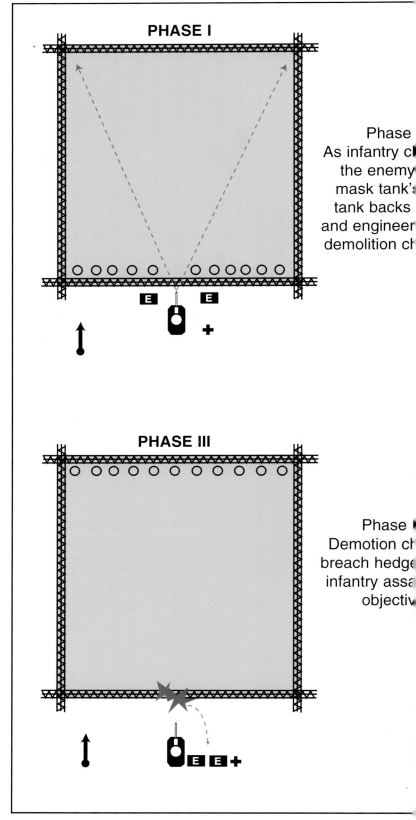

HEDGE-BUSTING TACTICS IN NORMANDY

PHASE II

Phase II
Tank lays down
suppressive fire
as infantry
clamber through
the hedgerow

 Sherman
tank

60mm
mortar

E Engineer team

○ Infantryman

+ Mortar
observer

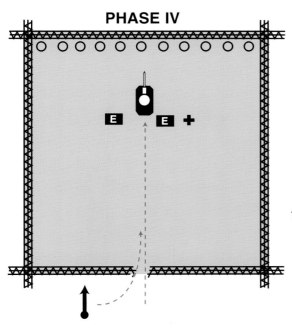

PHASE IV

Phase IV
Tank advances to
support infantry in
clearing the far
hedge. Other units
move forward from
the rear to continue
the attack

■ *Left:* Designed as an infantry support, antitank weapon, the turretless Sturmgeschütz (StuG) assault gun was best used, as here, defensively, behind good cover.

■ *Below:* The largest number of German tanks in Normandy were Mk IVs. This Ausf H carries a 75mm KwK gun with a range of 3000m (3200 yards).

■ *Right:* The plate armour on the turret of this Mk IV Ausf H was designed to explode hollow-charged enemy shells: plates were also fixed on the sides of hull. The patterning on the hull-front is made by *Zimmerit*, an anti-magnetic paste to defend against mines.

limited amount of space available in the beachhead – Bradley was determined to punch through LXXXIV Corps into the French countryside beyond.

Even prior to the brief halt in the fighting that took place in mid-June, individual American commanders were finding ways to deal with the

hedgerows. In fact, many of these methods had already been in use as the fighting ground to a temporary halt. The 29th Infantry Division was among the first US Army divisions to devise newer methods in busting through the hedgerows. Commanders at all levels in the division experimented with tactics

■ *Above:* The fighting at times could get this close. Men of the 119th Infantry Regiment around Mortain work in on an enemy sniper.

that emphasized close cooperation between tanks and infantry. In order to inculcate these lessons quickly with officers at all levels of command, division headquarters conducted rehearsals prior to an attack on how to smash through the hedgerows or avoid problems. Inevitably, however, these countermeasures fell short of the mark as US infantrymen and tankers applied standard prewar tank-infantry doctrine in combating the entrenched German positions in the hedgerows.

As for the tank-infantry teams, the armour on many occasions out-distanced the accompanying infantry: driving through the earthen barriers that had been breached with explosives

packed inside bangalore torpedo tubes mounted on the front of the armoured vehicles. After a gap in the hedgerow had been blown the tanks would then race into the next field, with the attacking infantry trailing behind without cover as they followed on through the breach. While German antitank gunners picked off the unescorted tanks with accurate fire, machine gunners either pinned down or annihilated the unprotected infantry piecemeal.

The 29th Division tried another method called fire and manoeuvre, something that the army had preached before and during World War II but seldom ever practised. In order to break the stalemate in the *bocage* country General Gerhardt, and his assistant division commander Brigadier-General Norman D. Cota, set out to create closely coordinated combat teams, not unlike the ones formed by the US

■ *Above:* When the Allied advance became too slow, then air power often offered a solution. These are the remains of St-Lô after an air attack. To the east, Caen was to suffer the same fate.

Marines in the Pacific to deal with the Japanese bunkers. The tactics developed by the 29th Division were a departure from normal doctrine in that neither the tanks nor the infantry led the attack, but fought closely together and protected one another while closing with the enemy. The solution both Gerhardt and Cota devised combined firepower with manoeuvre within small infantry-armour combat teams. These teams consisted of a single tank, engineer tank

and a squad of infantry reinforced by a light machine gun and a 60mm infantry mortar. After the team was formed up, and prior to the attack, the infantry and the engineers occupied the hedgerow opposite to the one that was about to be assaulted.

The conceptual idea for this tank-infantry team had its origins in the aftermath of the defeat at Kasserine Pass in February 1943 and in problems encountered during the fighting in Italy.

In fact, while the US Army's prewar *Field Service Regulations* called for close cooperation between the infantry and tanks, little was done by army planners to implement a sound tank-infantry doctrine until the fighting in the *bocage* in June 1944. Indeed, it was not until the stalemate in the *bocage* that army planners took serious the need for a sound tank-infantry doctrine. Only when US commanders were faced with stiff German resistance in the hedgerows did anyone contemplate the need for tanks supporting infantry in the assault.

In theory an attack on a defended hedgerow began first with a Sherman equipped with a main gun and machine guns. The Sherman fired a white

■ *Left:* This is how most hedgerows had to be taken – at a run with the hope that the Germans were not armed, ready and waiting on the other side of the field.

attacked when the Sherman opened fire with its machine guns. The squad moved through the hedgerow, deployed in line and advanced across the open field using standard methods of fire and movement. The infantry stayed away from hedgerows on their flanks in order to avoid enemy grazing fire. The Sherman continued to support the attack until the infantry's advance masked the tank's machine-gun fire. As they closed on the German positions, American infantrymen threw hand grenades over the hedgerow to kill or confuse German defenders on the opposite side. Simultaneously, the Sherman backed away from its firing position, and the engineers emplaced demolitions in the holes left by the Sherman's pipe devices. After the explosives blew a hole in the hedgerow, the Sherman moved forward to provide close support to the infantry squad. The tankers and infantrymen then flushed the hedgerow of any remaining defenders and prepared to continue the attack. The engineer team and machine gun and mortar crews then displaced forward to support the next assault. [5]

Tank-Infantry Cooperation

Another method used by American commanders to overcome the *bocage* was to improve tank-infantry coordination. While most Sherman tanks came with telephones mounted on the back deck of the tank and one inside the tank itself, this method of infantry-tank communications exposed the infantryman talking to the tank crew to enemy machine-gun or small-arms fire. One solution was to lengthen the telephone wire that enabled the

phosphorous round into the corners of the opposite hedgerow to eliminate German heavy machine-gun positions. The tankers then systematically put machine-gun fire along the entire base of the enemy hedgerow. The 60mm mortar supported the attack by lobbing shells into the fields directly behind the German positions. The infantry

infantryman to talk to the crew from a safer position. Once again, however, the cord either sometimes became caught up in the tank track and severed, or simply pulled or snapped loose. Army communications personnel solved this problem by mounting a tank interphone into an empty ammunition box and mounted it on the back deck of the Sherman. To talk to the tankers inside, all that an infantryman had to do was to insert a radio handset plug into the box and talk from a safe position in order to direct fire. By mid-July, as General Bradley prepared his breakout from Normandy, many divisions in the First Army had adopted such a method for tank-infantry communications.

Some tankers also installed infantry radio sets or acquired extra manpack radios for use by the infantry. Tactically, another method used by American infantry commanders was to ride inside tanks and direct unit attacks through the use of the manpack infantry radio sets. By employing such a method of command and control, commanders could simultaneously control and coordinate the tank-infantry team in the assault.

Infantrymen and tankers also developed a wide range of hand-held signals and standard operating procedures to improve tank-infantry coordination. Because each branch used different signals, tank-infantry teams invented signals for "Commence fire",

■ *Below:* Action around Cherbourg in mid-June. Mortars were usually attached to US infantry battalions in batteries of six, as part of a heavy weapons company.

■ *Right:* German infantry relied heavily on mortars in Normandy, having as many as 20 120mm mortars and 60 80mm weapons, such as this one, per division.

"Cease fire", and to point out enemy locations. Troops were designated to carry rifles equipped with tracer rounds to mark targets, while platoon and squad leaders carried smoke grenades or flares that signalled where tanks were to aim their fire.

Of all the devices devised to break the deadlock in the *bocage* none was as famous and well-publicized as that developed by Sergeant Curtis G. Culin of the 2nd Armored Division's 102nd Cavalry Reconnaissance Squadron. Taking to heart a suggestion that what the GIs needed was something to "cut through the hedgerows like teeth", Sergeant Culin designed just such a device from discarded German steel beach obstacles and fashioned them into a cutting device. After witnessing a

■ *Right:* As well as the Nebelwerfer static launcher, the Wehrmacht developed vehicle-mounted launchers for their rockets – such as this one.

successful field test whereby a Sherman tank mounted with Culin's cutting device easily ploughed through a hedgerow, General Bradley ordered the construction and installation of as many of the hedgerow cutters as possible. After assembling all the available welders and welding equipment in the division, as well as all the German scrap metal from the beachhead defences, the First Army's welding teams were able to provide American field commanders with over 500 hedgerow cutters or "rhino tanks" as the GIs referred to them, prior to the breakout from the *bocage* and the drive on St-Lô.[6] General Eisenhower specifically noted in his memoirs that the GIs were "gleeful" in the knowledge that both German steel and their defences were being turned against their former owners![7]

Hedge Busting

Tank crews of the 747th also came up with their own means of dealing with the hedgerows. Besides equipping tanks with bangalore torpedo-like tubes designed to punch two holes in the hedgerow, combat engineers then placed two 105mm shell casings packed with TNT into the holes and then ignited them.

This method had a downside, however, as the appearance of a Sherman tank with such devices signalled to the Germans that an attack was about to take place, and thus gave them time to direct their fire against the offending tank. First Lieutenant Charles B. Green countered this with his own idea of welding railway tracks on the front hulls of the Sherman tanks which enabled them to smash their way through the thickest hedgerows. Army

■ *Left:* The sure way of busting a hedgerow was to use a tank. A Stuart fitted with a "Rhino" ploughs through behind the advancing infantry.

combat engineers also developed a method of planting sandbags filled with explosives underneath an embankment. Once detonated, it blew a sizeable hole in the hedgerow that permitted a tank to pass through with following infantrymen.

Forward Artillery Observers

In order to assist the artillerymen, who likewise had become frustrated in providing the infantry and tanks with close-in artillery support, forward artillery observers were assigned to one rifle platoon per company, while tank commanders had one assigned to each company commander (a shortage of Forward Observers or "FOs" prompted greater reliance on aerial observation from the 10 light aircraft found in every division assigned for liaison missions). The FOs assigned to each company were thus better able to observe and call in fire missions against German positions when they were needed, since their radios were directly connected to the supporting artillery battery's fire direction centre. Because they could loiter for hours due to Allied air supremacy, the FOs "called fire on forward enemy positions and lucrative targets in the enemy rear and adjusted barrages in support of American ground attacks."[8] The light L-4 Piper Cubs and Stinson Sentinels, often called "bird dogs" by the American soldiers, also played their part by supporting fighter-bombers that flew overhead by identifying targets for close air support missions (when the weather allowed). In conclusion, in Normandy, aerial FOs conducted the majority of observed target fire missions with universally excellent results.

In the long run, however, "busting the *bocage*" would rely upon the development and efficiency of the combined-arms team in order to allow tankers and infantrymen to bring their firepower to bear on the enemy. Due to the fact that both Overlord and Neptune (the amphibious phase of D-Day) had consumed much of the attention of planners in London, little thought or preparation was given to the fighting that would take place beyond the beachhead.

This lapse in training for what turned out to be a war of attrition after the initial landings is all the more important in that hedgerows covered nearly 95 percent of the Cotentin Peninsula, stretching north from Utah Beach through Coutances to the port of Cherbourg. General Bradley's and his officers' surprise at the difficulty of the terrain forced a rapid re-evaluation of timetables as more and more men poured ashore from bases in England for the push into the interior of France.

■ *Above:* Of course many tanks never reached the other side of the field. This M–4 Sherman has been hit by shellfire in a German counterattack and looks as if it has been looted.

With a brief lull in the fighting towards the end of June, divisions such as the 29th experimented with tactics that would permit them to burst through the hedgerows and continue the attack towards St-Lô and beyond. The lessons learned in these rehearsals ultimately contributed to the US First Army's breakout from Normandy.

In one major exercise that tested the new "hedgerow-busting" tactics on 24 June 1944, soldiers of the 29th Division held a full attack rehearsal where they tested the new close assault tactics developed from the lessons learned. What the GIs discovered assisted them greatly a few weeks later when the First Army resumed the offensive towards St-Lô, and finally broke the German Seventh Army's defences.

In the 29th Division's rehearsal General Gerhardt sought to test the effectiveness of the new tactics and discovered that by using the assets already available, German positions in the hedgerows could be penetrated. Part of the new assault tactics practised was the use of a reinforced combat assault team made up of an infantry platoon, tank platoon and three engineer teams working in unison to break through the earthen banks. As the army's official history of the campaign in Normandy emphasized, here lay the key to victory in the hedgerows. In fact, the most obvious weakness of the American ground attack to date was the tank-infantry team. Many infantry commanders did not know how to use tanks properly in support, and many tank commanders did not realize how best to offer assistance to the accompanying infantry. As mentioned above, all of this had been written and lectured about during the interwar era at the Infantry School at Fort Benning, Georgia, and the Command and Staff College at Fort Leavenworth, Kansas, as one of the most important lessons of the US Army's campaign in World War I; namely, the emergence of the combined-arms attack. In fact, as a US Army operational assessment concluded before the war, though this was largely

■ *Right:* This MG42 team are wearing Waffen-SS panzer camouflage uniforms, so may well be members of a panzergrenadier company of one of the SS panzer divisions.

ignored as fighting actually commenced: "The development of operational procedures and techniques between the infantry and close support tanks must not be left until the arrival at the combat zone."[9] General Bradley and other American commanders soon discovered that the infantry divisions had received insufficient training with separate tank battalions. What is not acknowledged is the fact that this situation existed due to the army's *Field Service Regulations*, and the organization of the triangular infantry division just prior to the World War II, which omitted inclusion of a tank battalion in its table of organization.

Infantry Weapons

As for the infantrymen themselves, one of the most important lessons learned was that they could not use their .3in-calibre machine guns "quickly enough" to provide close-in support during an assault. Instead, the infantry discovered that the BAR offered the best support because it was portable enough to follow the attack through and could provide a blanket of fire to suppress enemy machine guns and small-arms fire. For their part, mortar crews discovered that they could use the rear deck of the Sherman tank as an observation platform in order to adjust their rounds onto German positions. They also learned that they could best protect the infantry by lobbing smoke shells in front of German observation ports. Above all else, both infantry and tank commanders now emphasized better coordination of their efforts in order to protect better the assaulting infantry. One last lesson learned was avoidance of

Not all the fighting took place in the fields: the town of Valognes was all but levelled after German counterattacks to defend Cherbourg.

■ *Right:* The view of Cherbourg from the Fort du Roule battery, as US infantry clear a way towards the heart of the vital Atlantic port.

enfilading fire along the axis whereby in the past squads and platoons had been too often pinned down by German automatic fire that had been set up in field corners in anticipation of an American attack. In order to avoid this deadly fire, Brigadier-General Norman D. Cota, the 29th's assistant divisional commander, introduced a new procedure whereby infantrymen would advance across the open centres of the hedge-bordered fields rather than moving along the axial hedgerows. General Cota's new tactics were, in fact, put to the test starting on 11 July whereby a local attack would commence with small teams operating on a broad front, with one squad of infantry and one tank per field, and a squad of combat engineers with explosives assigned to each infantry platoon, in order to break the deadlock.

Problems on the Ground

The difficulty of on-the-spot coordination between an infantry platoon leader taking cover in a ditch and a commander buttoned up in his tank was a continual complaint that would hinder the relationship between tank crews and infantrymen. Because voice command could not always be heard above the sounds of battle and the noises of tank motors, hand signals had to be worked out and smoke signals and pyrotechnic devices pre-arranged. Riflemen guiding tanks sometimes had to get out in front and sometimes actually jump up and down in order to attract the attention of members of the tank crew. Eventually, a tanker would carefully stick his head out to take the message. Because armour and infantry

■ *Above:* Cherbourg fell to the First Army on 1 July. The wreckage and dead of both sides around Fort du Roule show it was not without heavy cost.

radios operated on different channels and frequencies, division signals companies installed infantry-type radios in the tanks that could be turned to the net used by the infantry. Signals men also installed microphones or telephones connected to the tank's intercom system that eventually resolved the communications problems between the infantry and the tankers, though it was nevertheless a slow and painful learning process.[10]

As the infantrymen and tankers worked out their problems during the last week in June, prior to the commencement of Bradley's push towards St-Lô-Coutances, combat engineers refined their demolition procedures in order to blast tank-sized openings in the hedgerows and earth banks. They also practised assembling bridging sections and pontoons for crossing rivers and canals.

One last effort by American commanders to prepare their men was the adoption of more aggressive combat tactics. As General Bradley and others discovered during the fighting throughout June, American troops tended to "bunch up" or quickly hit the ground whenever German fire opened up, thereby bringing the attack to a halt. This combination of mistakes inevitably led to more casualties as the GIs offered themselves as targets to enemy snipers, as well as allowing the Germans time to withdraw or bring up reinforcements. One US platoon commander recalled an attack on a hedgerow after a lone German sniper had killed a soldier as he advanced towards a suspected enemy position, the remaining members of his squad hit the deck not knowing where the sniper was located or where the fire had come from. The sniper then proceeded to pick each soldier off individually. With incidents such as these in mind, US commanders attempted with some success to indoctrinate their men with the idea that the best way to stay alive was a continuous and aggressive advance.

Private First Class Leon C. Standifer, a member of the first squad, Company

K, 376th Infantry Regiment, 94th Division, recalled that such a stance did not imply that a GI was not not scared:

"My mind was running through options. If I turned around to walk back the gunner would fire. Flanking was impossible. 'Yea, though I walk through the valley of the shadow of death, I will fear no evil.' My muscles were tense, my hands were sweaty – the rifle felt slippery, I slid the safety lock off and walked straight at the gun, boldly and aggressively but very carefully.... At thirty yards I stopped to my knee.

"The gunner would open up somewhere between here and 10 yards. I couldn't see a thing. Where would the enemy riflemen be. There was no cover close to the shed. Rifles would be along that hedgerow. . . . I thought, 'Leon, you're stalling.'

"The squad is watching. I came up to a crouch, rifle ready from the hip. Cut every thought out of your mind. Depend on instinct. Fire at any sound or motion, anywhere.... Twenty yards. At this range he couldn't miss. I might get one round off. I stopped 10 yards from the shed. I could see nothing

■ *Above:* **Areas of German resistance remained on the Cotentin Peninsula into July. The rifle grenade (centre) is a Type M9A1.**

■ *Above:* The defeated enemy. Captured members of the Cherbourg garrison include both army and Luftwaffe ground troops.

through the hole. Maybe there wasn't a gun. I reached the shed and opened the door. Just a few tools. I poked through some brush and signalled the patrol. Nothing happened, but to survive as a scout, you have to stay scared." [11]

For the exercise held on 24 June 1944, coordination of infantry-tank-engineer teams, working in small groups, had been carefully rehearsed.

The tanks were expected to give greater assistance through use of their firepower in dealing with the German defences. But still there remained the problem of getting the tanks (and infantry) through the earthen embankments, fast enough to maintain their support through the endless series of fields. Movement along the roads and lanes was almost impossible, as German troops armed with antitank guns and panzerfausts

were skilfully positioned to deal with American armour. In tactics rehearsed throughout the last week of June and first week of July 1944, infantrymen would seize hedgerows fronting the axis of attack, a tank would then lumber forward towards a place where the engineers desired to make the gap. Driving into the hedgerow, the "rhino" tank fitted with its steel cutting blades would force the two prongs into the earth, and at the same time deliver a blast of fire from its automatic weapons on the field and hedgerow ahead. When the prongs were withdrawn from the bank, two waiting engineers would rush forward, place the prepared demolition charges in the holes made by the tank, make the necessary primer connections, light the fuze, "and run like hell", as one combat engineer recalled.

Additional TNT charges were carried close behind the assault in M-29 "Weasels", an amphibious prime carrier used to transport extra equipment and men over swampy or rough terrain. The engineers, in fact, had perhaps the most dangerous and difficult jobs of all of the members of the assault teams. Not only did they carry the explosives, but they had to set them off: an unenviable task at the best of times. Coupled with this was the obvious fact that they had had to concentrate on the job at hand and not worry about enemy infantry. Here, the engineers relied on both the tanks and infantry for protective fire.

As was often the case, however, in absence of an accompanying attack by tanks, the only way to tell if a hedgerow was occupied by Germans prior to its demolition was to approach it from a frontal position with little or no cover. Private First Class Standifer, whom we met earlier, recalled such an instance as his squad cleared the town of Hirgoat they then entered a group of hedgerows: "The patrol formed along the first hedgerow. I climbed over it and started towards the next, about 30 yards away. It had brush growing all along the top. At any point [it] could hide a machine gun but the middle was the best bet, with riflemen on each side. I walked that field as I had done in the valley and reached the hedgerow without a shot. I climbed up at a clear spot and saw there was nobody on the other side. Then I looked to the next hedgerow. It had a break in it, and I saw movement beyond"[12]

Fortunately, as Private First Class Standifer noted, the Germans in this particular hedgerow were part of a patrol that shortly afterwards moved out. They did so without having spotted either him or his fire team. In fact, not noticing the Americans, the Germans continued talking to their comrades who were manning a machine-gun position, flanked by two rifles on either side, exactly as Standifer had predicted.

Summary

By the beginning of July, those Americans who had survived the landings at Omaha and Utah and the subsequent fight for Cherbourg and the area outside of St-Lô had no illusions as to the forthcoming fight to break out of the *bocage*. The tactics introduced by Gerhardt and Cota were testimony to a stubborn German Army that was increasingly on the defensive. As the fight for St-Lô proved, the Americans were a long way off in overcoming the terrain, and the German forces that were now reinforced by parachute and assault troops were determined to carry out Adolf Hitler's strategy of attrition "to the last man".

Even as the 29th Division prepared to resume the St-Lô offensive, the effectiveness of Cota's new tactics were about to undergo a severe test.

CHAPTER IV:

"THE FIGHT FOR THE HEDGEROWS" PHASE TWO

The German dispositions for the defence of St-Lô. The US First Army strikes south from Cherbourg and east of St-Lô, but faces an ever-worsening battle of attrition.

Even as V Corps prepared for its push inland toward St-Lô and Coutances, General Omar N. Bradley outlined his plans of operation to break out of the Normandy lodgement area and into the interior of France beyond St-Lô. Faced with stiffening resistance and the reinforcement of German defences in Normandy, now led by Field Marshal Guenther von Kluge,[1] who had succeeded von Rundstedt on 4 July, the US First Army prepared to advance into the heart of hedgerow country and force a breakout. The need for this was becoming increasingly urgent as more and more American troops were arriving in France and the area under First Army control was not yet big enough to allow the activation of the US Third Army under General George S. Patton.

For the average American rifleman, this meant more of the same: row after row of hedgerows occupied by a steadfast German defender determined to fight for every inch of

■ *Left:* Members of a US First Army pioneer company prepare a howitzer emplacement. A battery of six howitzers operated in support of infantry battalions. Artillery batteries also operated at brigade and corps level.

ground in order to prevent the Americans from advancing towards Germany's borders, over terrain that was marked not only by the earthen fortresses but in fields turned into quagmires by a steady rain that began in early July just as the American attack commenced.

The Hedgerows Fight: July 1944

According to General Bradley, once the port of Cherbourg had been taken, the "way was cleared for the Allied offensive that was to be initiated by a breakout. The basic strategy for this attack out of the lodgement had been written into the Overlord plan. France was to be liberated in phases and we now stood at the brink of the first: a swift push from the grassy pasture lands of Normandy to the sleepy banks of the Seine."[2]

The forces that were to achieve this breakout were Major-General Troy H. Middleton's VIII Corps and Lieutenant-General Joseph L. Collins' VII Corps, both of whose forces had been up against a determined adversary for weeks. The first objectives of General Bradley's First Army was to seize the town of St-Lô and its vital road junction and then swing east towards the River Seine, with the liberation of Paris being the primary goal of this first major US Army offensive in Northwest Europe.

■ *Above:* Major-General Troy H. Middleton (right) commander of VIII Corps. In July he would take his corps south down the west coast of the Cotentin, through Lessay and Ducey, breaking out into Brittany on 3 August.

As General Bradley admitted, this was no easy task as any chance to wage a war of mobility would require that the First Army force a breakout as opposed to merely pushing the Germans aside. Bradley admitted that only a breakout would "enable us to crash into the enemy's rear where we could fight a war of movement on our own best terms. As long as the enemy confined us to the *bocage* of Normandy where we were forced to match him man for man, he could exact a prohibitive price for the few miserable yards we might gain." (Bradley, *A Soldier's Story*) General Bradley reasoned that if any breakout were to occur, it must be directed towards an enemy "soft spot" where US forces could be concentrated against it, and "smash" their way through a gap with such a heavy blow that it would crush his frontline defences. This would then enable divisions to pour through the gap before the Germans could regain their balance.

■ *Right:*
Lieutenant-General Joseph L. Collins, commander of VII Corps. Collins got his men to the west coast of the Cotentin on 18 June and had taken Cherbourg by the end of the month. Turning south, VII Corps broke through to Carentan, Periérs and turned east to form the southern edge of the Falaise Pocket in mid-August.

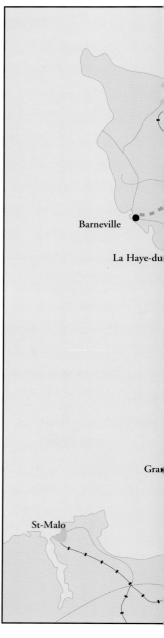

The spot chosen the breakthrough was, "somewhere along the sixteen-mile line between St-Lô and Coutances". Even General Bradley admitted that this would not be easy as German resistance would make the likelihood of a push from there across to Coutances "very costly". The second alternative for the First Army was to force its way out of the Cotentin Peninsula from the vicinity of Carentan and through some of the most difficult terrain in the region (primarily swampy marshland) before reaching the agreed-upon breakout line. After careful examination of this terrain, Bradley and his staff believed it also too costly.

The third alternative and the one chosen was a drive that led straight down the west coast Cotentin road from La Haye-du-Puits through the moors of

■ Above left: The defence of St-Lô was in the hands of the élite 3rd Parachute Division. It was one of the first German divisions to reach the Normandy area after D-Day.

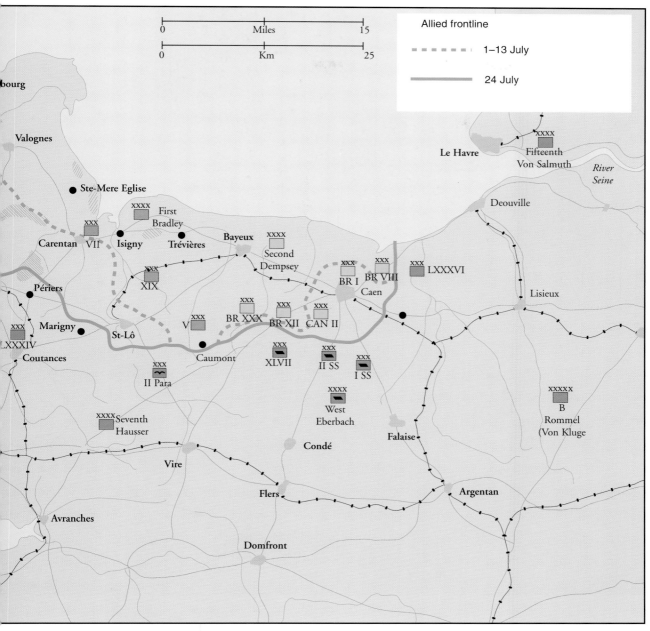

Lessay to Coutances. Bradley wrote that: "If we could break into Coutances from the west coast road, the enemy would be forced to withdraw across the rest of the Cotentin neck for fear of being cut off by a pincer attack from St-Lô." (Bradley, ibid) With the St-Lô-Coutances road designated as the line of departure American forces would thus be in a position to initiate the breakout from the *bocage* country.

With the adaptation of such a strategy, General Middleton's VIII Corps was to lead the attack down the west coast road while General Collins' VII Corps was to take over a portion of Middleton's front across the Carentan marshes and push the Germans out through the neck as Middleton's forces continued advancing towards Coutances. Field Marshal Montgomery, meanwhile, was to renew the offensive towards Caen

■ *Above:* The expansion of the Allied beachhead in July saw offensives along the whole of the front except in the US V Corps' sector area around Caumont.

■ *Above:* The Zugmachine halftrack tractor mounting 20mm AA guns. In 1944 there were six of these vehicles in each panzer division: three per battalion staff company.

in the British and Canadian sectors in order to take some pressure off Bradley's First Army. What Generals Bradley, Collins and Middleton discovered, however, was that the Germans had had sufficient time to reinforce substantially their positions.

By the end of June, the German Army in the West had been reinforced, with elements of the 2nd SS Panzer Division already in positions around St-Lô. In fact, the Germans had observed

the American offensive preparations from the heights surrounding La Haye-du-Puits, and as the US Army's official history noted, "they were ready". After a reshuffling of their forces in the Seventh Army, Rommel had managed, through great effort, to assemble a force that was able to defend in-depth. Immediately opposing Middleton's VIII Corps was Group *Koenig*, commanded by Colonel Eugen Koenig, which comprised the 91st, 265th and 243rd Divisions on the

flanks, and a large contingent of *Osttruppen*, made up of conscripts from non-Germanic Eastern European countries and former Russian prisoners of war, holding the centre.

The Germans had, besides the services of the 2nd SS Panzer Division, an adequate force of artillery at their disposal. This included the artillery of the 243rd Division, two cannon companies, five antitank companies, a complete tank-destroyer battalion, and an assortment of howitzers, rocket launchers, antiaircraft batteries, captured Russian guns and several old French light tanks. Positioned behind Group *Koenig* was the 352nd Division and a battle group from the 77th Division. These last two units were to defend the high ground of the Montgarden Ridge and Monte Castre. The 2nd SS Panzer Division, strategically positioned south of St-Lô in reserve, was to act as a mobile reaction force and prevent any breakthrough or act as a blocking force near La Hay-du-Puits. Closer in was the 15th Parachute Regiment from the 5th Parachute Division, which was still in Brittany. In sum, the Germans had managed to stabilize the front and were not about to cede any ground without a hard fight.

First Army Resumes the Offensive

As Field Marshal Montgomery noted in his wartime memoirs, his main order to General Bradley (as nominal commander of Allied ground forces before the breakout) was to emphasize the need for speed in starting the drive to the south, to take advantage of the existing enemy dispositions to stage the breakout quickly. While Montgomery's Twenty-First Army Group renewed the offensive towards Caen to divert attention away from Bradley's First Army, the Americans, primarily Collins'

VII Corps, were to strike out of the hedgerows and after seizing St-Lô head towards Falaise and Argentan in order to commence the drive to the Seine and the liberation of Paris. This would create space for the activation of Lieutenant-General George S. Patton's Third Army, whose tanks were to break out west to capture Brittany and its Atlantic ports. As it transpired, only two Third Army corps (VIII and XIX) were tasked with this, as, in a move which the *bocage* fighting had held up for weeks, Patton and the rest of his army broke out from Avranches into France on 3 August, driving south and east to reach the River Loire on 16 August and the Seine east of Paris on the 25th.

The British field marshal noted that, "before General Bradley could launch his breakout operation in strength, he had to undertake difficult and laborious preliminary operations to secure a suitable starting position". As Montgomery and Bradley both discovered, the Germans remained committed to the defence of Normandy and would deny them an easy breakout from their lodgement areas.

Stiff Resistance

Despite the massive reinforcements that arrived from England via gliders and the attachment of the 82nd Airborne Division, commanded by Brigadier-General Matthew B. Ridgway, to VIII Corps for the offensive, which commenced on 3 July, the Americans once again ran into stiff resistance along the Poterie Ridge-Monte Castre axis. For nearly four days, the glider-borne US infantry slugged it out with the Germans, and after sustaining extremely heavy casualties, the 82nd Airborne Division finally succeeded in cracking the Wehrmacht's main line of defence.

As the paratroopers attacked Hill 95 on 3 July, the 79th and 90th Infantry

Divisions attacked towards Monte Castre, where, in drenching rain, the 90th struck out towards Monte Castre through the hedgerows and the heavily wooded slopes with the intended goal of linking up with the 79th Division. In the assault on Monte Castre, Major-General Eugene M. Landrum, the commanding general of the 90th Division, brought down a large amount of fire support for the infantry in the way of corps artillery, tanks, assault guns and tank destroyers in order to overwhelm the German defenders. After nearly two hours into the attack, in which it appeared that the 90th was making progress, the advance bogged down as German resistance increased. In fact, on the first day of this attack the 90th Division advanced less than 1.6km (one mile) on 3 July with a cost of over 600 casualties. The Germans demonstrated, rather convincingly, that they intended and were able to make a stand. In reality, the 90th Division's attack dented only the outpost line of resistance and had yet to make contact with the main defences. As one officer of the 90th stated: "The Germans haven't much left, but they sure as hell know how to use it."

American Deficiencies

The problem, however, was not just a stiffening of the Germans' resistance. Part of the problem remained with the inability of the tank crews and infantrymen to work closely together in smashing through the hedgerows. Other problems also existed regarding the command and control of the attacking infantrymen, as well as overall fire discipline as "jumpy" riflemen fired at the slightest movement or sound in the

■ *Left:* The *Panzerfausts* this Waffen-SS soldier carries were the first one-shot antitank weapon ever developed.

hedgerows. In one local German counterattack, for example, as American troops entered the hamlet of les Sablons, several German tracked vehicles appeared from behind nearby hedgerows. In the attack, a near panic ensued as the infantrymen fled the town. In order to restore order and maintain the momentum of the advance, Colonel Richard C. Partridge committed his reserve battalion as well as bringing forward three assault guns and three platoons of the regimental antitank company to guard against enemy armour. Eventually, the soldiers of 358th Infantry Regiment were able to break German resistance and push through the town.

Troubles for the 90th Division, however, continued as both the rain and German resistance, in the form of an extremely accurate artillery barrage, managed to pin down elements of the division. Eventually, after attempting to outflank the German defences atop Monte Castre, and the commitment of the division reserves, the 359th Infantry Regiment, along with a tactical air strike and artillery fire, four battalions of the 90th (three from the 359th and one from the 358th) eventually occupied not only Monte Castre but the adjoining Hill 122 on the evening of 6 July.

Despite being thrown off Monte Castre and Hill 122, the Germans counterattacked repeatedly on the evening of 6/7 July, though the 90th Division tenaciously held on to its hilltop positions. Meanwhile, elements of Colonel George H. Barth's 357th Infantry Regiment struck out towards the village of Beaucoudray. Aided by artillery, infantry and tanks, Barth's men entered the corridor on 5 July and destroyed a self-propelled gun and moved to within 914m (1000 yards) of Beaucoudray before German artillery and mortar fire turned it back. Here, the men of the 357th sought cover in the

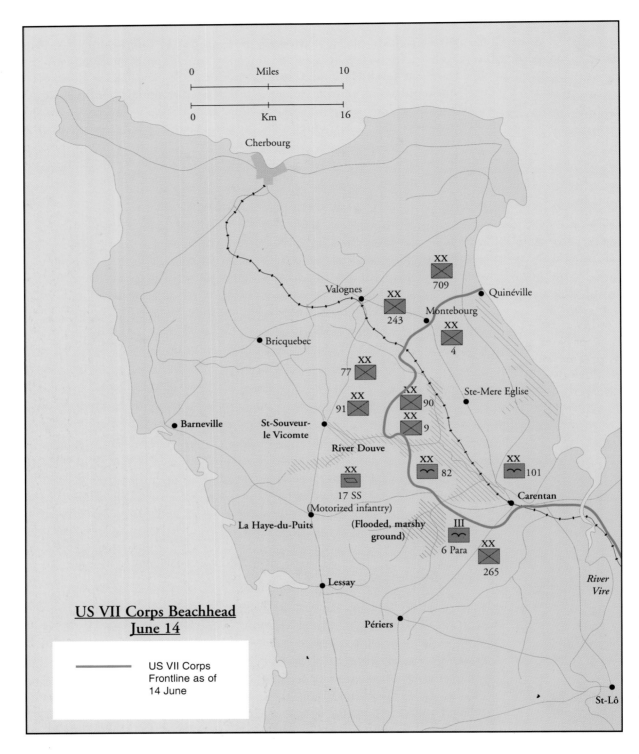

US VII Corps Beachhead
June 14

US VII Corps
Frontline as of
14 June

adjoining hedgerows where the German infantry continued to fire on them.

Colonel Barth renewed the attack on the morning of 6 July as a rifle company, assisted by artillery and smoke shells, advanced through Beaucoudray. Meanwhile, two more rifle companies provided cover fire for two other rifle companies several hundred yards south of the village. With these additional units

■ *Above:* The VII Corps frontline 16km (10 miles) beyond Utah Beach.

this gave Colonel Barth a total of five rifle companies in position to resume the advance towards the division's objective.

The soldiers of the 357th were in a vulnerable position as the Germans, reinforced by the 15th Parachute Regiment and the last elements of the Seventh Army's reserves, prepared to counterattack. In the late evening hours of 6 July, at 23:15 hours, the Germans struck as their artillery and mortars pounded the right flank of Barth's positions. While one company of Barth's northern group was able to beat back the German attack, the two rifle companies to the south of Beaucoudray were in serious danger of being cut off from the rest of the group.

■ *Right:* The engine of a Mk IV panzer under repair. Each panzer division had its own workshop company, consisting of platoons devoted to tank recovery; armoury; signals and spare parts resupply.

To alleviate the pressure on the southern group, Colonel Barth launched a counterattack supported by another rifle company and two platoons of medium tanks. Despite heavy mortar and machine-gun fire, the infantry reached the last hedgerow at the northern edge of Beaucoudray. There, the infantry company commander committed his supporting tanks against the Germans who had positioned themselves in the adjoining hedgerows. As the attack commenced, the company commander was struck by German fire. Meanwhile, the Germans launched a small counterattack against the American right flank. By this time all commissioned and noncommissioned officers had been either killed or wounded, such was the ferocity of enemy fire. Deprived of leadership, the infantrymen and tank crews fell back across the muddy fields to the assembly area. Heavy German fire prevented any further attempts to relieve the GIs cut off in Beaucoudray.

Eventually, the rifle company that had been cut off was forced to surrender as the German tanks overran its command post inside the town, thus ending all further attempts by Colonel Barth to rescue the defenders in Beaucoudray.

After nearly five days of combat the 90th Division had advanced about 6.4km (four miles) at the cost of over 2000 casualties, a considerably high price for such small gains. While the leadership of the 90th Division came into question, the simple truth of the matter was that the division had been

■ *Right:* Deep in a foxhole a young infantry *schütze* (private) scans the skies for Allied aircraft. By June 1944 the Luftwaffe had all but disappeared from the skies of France, leaving German ground troops under constant aerial threat.

assigned a difficult mission to start with. Attacking over difficult terrain that the enemy had skilfully organized, and which was stubbornly defended by a German Army that was equal if not superior in numbers (approximately 5600 frontline combat troops of the 91st, 265th, 77th and 353rd Infantry Divisions, and the 15th Parachute Regiment), the 90th Division's attack had forced the commander of the German Seventh Army to call up his remaining reserves for this last-ditch defensive effort. In fact, while critics have since blamed Major-General Landham for his division's lack of aggressiveness and its inability to absorb the lessons of earlier hedgerow fighting

and disseminate them throughout the entire division, the failure to secure its initial objectives south of La-Haye-du-Puits and Beaucoudray was not what troubled higher commanders. General Bradley and the other senior American commanders were instead more concerned that the division seemed to "come to a halt" in its efforts to advance.

Just opposite the 90th was the 79th Division. Commanded by Major-General Ira T. Wyche, the 79th had been assigned the task of taking Montgardon Ridge and driving towards La Haye-du-Puits. With rifle companies assigned to each side of the road, machine-gun and mortar fire from a nearby railway embankment halted the

■ *Above:* At long range, German artillery engage American units in July. Once again, fear of air attack swathes the gun in camouflage, though even this might prove insufficient to fool the roaming squadrons of Allied fighter-bombers.

lead units until a soldier, Pfc William Thurston, charged the embankment and eliminated the enemy machine gunners with his M1 Garand rifle. Pfc Thurston's actions resulted in the "unhinging" of the German defences, with the lead elements of the division being able to advance 4.8km (three miles) towards their objective at Hill 121. For his actions during this battle Pfc Thurston was awarded the Army's Distinguished Service Cross.

After advancing towards Hill 121, the 314th Infantry Regiment set about to surround its objective and attack the summit of Montgardon Ridge. Colonel Warren A. Robinson, commanding officer of the 314th, using initiative, advanced against the German positions, and after a brief battle took the top of the ridge. On 4 July Colonel Robinson radioed General Wyche that Hill 121 was

secure. The 79th now had an observation post for its artillery forward observers to direct fire on La Haye-du-Puits.

Major-General Wyche also ordered the 315th Infantry forward. Once again the appearance of three German tanks along the road slowed its progress, as the armour prompted panic with the American infantrymen streaming to the rear in confusion. It was not until mid-afternoon on 3 July that the soldiers of the 315th and their supporting tanks were sufficiently reorganized to resume the advance. By nightfall, the 315th had advanced only 1.6km (one mile). Once again commanders blamed the hedgerows towards Montgardon. Nonetheless, the 314th's seizure of Hill 121 greatly assisted the 315th's advance which on 4 July made greater progress.

The Germans had not yet attempted a counterattack. Suddenly, however, on

■ *Below:* A 50mm PAK AT gun positioned on a main road with a clear field of fire against Allied armour. The rigidly built Normandy villages made ideal strongpoints from which the Germans could organize their lines of defence.

the evening of 4 July, with the infantrymen of the 315th only 3.2km (two miles) short of Hill 84, the Germans launched an assault. Infantry supported by Mk IV tanks and halftracks suddenly emerged from the hedgerows and quickly surrounded two of the 315th's rifle companies, which then were able to repulse the attack. Supported by the division's artillery on top of Hill 121, the regiment built up a solid defensive perimeter and prevented a German breakthrough.

After the 314th Infantry had seized La Hayes-du-Puits on 5 July 1944, General Wyche decided upon a new, bold move which he hoped might drive the division out of its slow hedgerow-by-hedgerow advance and perhaps in the process capture a sizeable number of Germans. By committing his reserve regiment, the 313th Infantry, General Wyche had hoped to conduct a wide envelopment to the right in order to pass across the western end of the Montgardon Ridge and drive rapidly downhill to the River Ay. The attack started at noon with a two-company tank-infantry task force in the lead. Once again marshy terrain, as well as the numerous hedgerows, slowed the movement of the attacking force. By late afternoon, the task force was still several hundred yards short of its objective. Here, it ran into such a heavy concentration of German fire that the attack stalled. At dusk, the Germans launched a violent counterattack and were able to drive the task force back several miles before calling off the attack. This respite gave the 313th time to regroup.

Having anticipated the inability of his other two regiments to break through the German defences, General Wyche ordered the battle-tested 315th back into action. On 5 July, the attack commenced against Hill 84 with the assistance of tanks and tank destroyers. This time the regiment reached the northern slope of the hill. The 79th finally had a toehold on the highest part of the Montgardon Ridge.

To reinforce its positions and prepare for the final conquest of Montgardon Ridge, General Wyche shuffled his two other regiments and ordered the 314th to swing to its right around La Haye-du-Puits and gain a foothold on the eastern slopes. The regiment quickly overcame German resistance that morning and achieved its objective. He then re-directed the efforts of the 313th eastwards from its location on the division's right rear to positions in support of the troop on Hill 84. By noon on 6 July, the fourth day of the attack, the 314th and 315th had managed to reach the northern and eastern slopes of Montgardon, while the 313th was echeloned to the right rear at the base of the ridge.

La Haye-du-Puits

In order to deal more effectively with German resistance in the hedgerows, General Wyche told each of his infantry commanders to attack alone when ready. The technique worked, as both the 314th and 315th managed to secure their objectives and complete the occupation of the eastern half of Montgardon Ridge. While the 313th Infantry ran up against stubborn German resistance, the 315th succeeded in taking Hill 84, while the 314th completed the occupation of Montgardon Ridge. During the morning of 7 July, German resistance crumbled as they withdrew towards the River Ay.

Despite these setbacks, the Germans still held the upper hand as the 79th Division once again ran up against savage resistance. In fact, the enemy re-entered La Haye-du-Puits. Meanwhile, Lieutenant-General Dietrich von Choltitz, commanding general of the 2nd SS Panzer Division *Das Reich*, launched his counterattack on the

■ *Left:* By 1944 the US Army had largely rejected the idea of towed AT guns because of their lack of mobility and usefulness in offence. Instead self-propelled "tank destroyers" were developed such the M-10, seen here. In the fighting around St-Lô two M-10s were attached per infantry battalion. The M-10 with its 3in gun was superceded by the M-18 "Hellcat" and the M-36.

■ *Right:* The sheer size and depth of the *bocage* hedges often meant that rifle grenades had to be used to dislodge a single German sniper.

afternoon of 7 July as an armoured contingent of two German battalions slammed into the 79th Division on the Montgardon Ridge. This German counterattack struck with such ferocity that the 79th was nearly pushed off the ridge. Recovering quickly from the initial shock of the German attack, General Wyche organized his force of infantry, tanks, tank destroyers and artillery into an effective combined-arms team with the result that the American soldiers were able to put up an effective and coordinated defence. After General Wyche's men destroyed three German tanks the attack began to lose its momentum. By nightfall on the 7th, von Choltitz's attack had been contained but so too was the earlier belief that the 79th could quickly advance to the River Ay.

Divisional Losses

As the US Army's official history noted, only after five days of savage fighting in the hedgerows were the soldiers of the 79th Division able to capture Montgardon Ridge. While the division suffered very few casualties during the first few days of the offensive, the German counterattack resulted in nearly 1000 US soldiers killed, wounded or missing. Total casualties for the division was over 2000 officers and enlisted men. Even more important, the 79th had been seriously depleted in the number of combat-effective troops, with some of its units being so demoralized that they had to be temporarily pulled from the line to refit and reorganize before resuming the offensive.[6]

In initiating the First Army's offensive, VIII Corps had failed to

achieve the breakout both Field Marshal Montgomery and General Bradley wanted. The Germans had clearly shown that they were fully prepared and determined to resist any further advance. They had given up very little ground, had defended their hedgerow positions with great tactical skill, had employed their weapons on a scale not anticipated by the Americans, and, most importantly, had inflicted a large number of casualties on the First Army's 79th and 90th Divisions. Furthermore the fighting for Montgardon Ridge clearly pointed to the fact that the Wehrmacht had not totally collapsed.

Combat Performance

As for VIII Corps, the failure to reach St-Lô created a further setback to the timetable for the impending drive to the Seine. Yet this was no fault of the 79th or 90th Divisions. While historians have been critical of their leadership and of the soldiers themselves, they have failed to take into consideration the fact that both American divisions were up against crack German troops defending well-organized and effective defensive positions, and that both outfits had managed to breach the German Army's main line of resistance. Having been fed untested replacements unfamiliar with hedgerow fighting, the performance of both divisions was bound to suffer. On the other hand, the divisions can be faulted for their failure to inculcate these same troops with the lessons of fighting the Germans in hedgerow country. Nonetheless, the point was clear that the Germans could "expect no respite" from the First Army's preliminary moves to force a breakout from the *bocage*. Even as the 79th and 90th Divisions were pulled from the lines, and the 82nd Airborne Division returned to England, the US VII Corps took up positions previously occupied by these units.

In keeping with General Eisenhower's and Field Marshal Montgomery's desire to keep the American attack to the south going, General Bradley ordered VII Corps to redeploy from Cherbourg to Carentan in order for it to assume operational responsibility for an area on the east (left) of VIII Corps. VII Corps was to assume the sector between the Prairies Marécageuses de Gorges (an area of swampland) and the flooded River Taute. This area was critical to the First

Army, as the only highway linking the US troops in the Cotentin with other Allied forces east of the River Taute passed through Carentan.

This sector was vulnerable: several German counterattacks nearly succeeded in taking the town and cutting the Allied beachhead into two. Likewise, any German breakthrough might sever the land communications between the Allies (British and Canadians). By advancing the frontline south of Carentan American forces would eliminate these dangers.

■ *Above:* The *bocage* was not the only obstacle the First Army had to contend with. Large areas behind Utah Beach were deliberately flooded by the German defenders.

More important, however, was the fact that VII Corps had as its objective a portion of the Coutances-St-Lô highway that served as a major causeway over the marshy terrain. Seizure of the Périers-St-Lô road was necessary in order to give VII Corps adequate room to deploy its forces in order to reach a junction with Middleton's VIII Corps.

As German resistance crumbled and VII and VIII Corps came together, General Bradley had hoped to use an armoured division that he had in army reserve to exploit American successes and break out of the hedgerow country.

General Bradley's attack in early July had been designed to seize the ground necessary, and as Field Marshal

■ *Right: SS-Generaloberst* **Paul Hausser took over the Seventh Army on 30 June after the death – from a heart attack – of Dollman.**

Montgomery knew, it would set the stage for the eventual breakout from the Normandy pocket. General Bradley's goal was not only to seize ground in order for the First Army to manoeuvre, but more importantly to gain control of the access to the Coutances-Marigny-St-Lô line, whereby he could then hold the positions necessary for the eventual breakout and not have to fight over the narrow, marshy terrain that dominated the approaches to St-Lô.

Bradley's Plan

Bradley's attack plan called for an effort that would begin on the right, near the sea, then widen progressively eastward in a series of blows by three of the four corps in line, with each corps attacking when ordered to do so. To reach the St-Lô objective would involve an advance of some 32km (20 miles) on the right flank, while the whole front would pivot on V Corps, east of St-Lô. The first part of this offensive was VIII Corps' offensive towards La Hay-du-Puits and the Monte Castre hills with three divisions (79th, 90th and 82nd Airborne). With the withdrawal of the 82nd Airborne from the battle in Normandy, General Bradley ordered the 8th Division from corps reserve to enter the battle along with VII Corps. Here, Major-General J. L. "Lightning Joe" Collins' VII Corps was to pick up the attack, with the 83rd and 4th Divisions acting as the lead elements while the 9th Infantry Division was to join the battle when the former two divisions had gained sufficient room to manoeuvre. Finally, XIX Corps would join the battle, aided by the 2nd Division of V Corps, in an area that included the River Vire, and would be aimed at the St-Lô area on both sides of that river. XIX Corps' 29th and 30th Divisions, and ultimately the 35th (still en route to France via the United States) would reinforce VII Corps' attack. The 3rd Armored Division was initially in army reserve, near Isigny.

The German order of battle in and around St-Lô constituted the larger part of Seventh Army and was commanded

by *SS-Generaloberst* Paul Hausser, who had succeeded Colonel-General Friedrich Dollman upon the latter's death on 29 June 1944 at his headquarters. Two corps, LXXXIV and II Parachute, held the front from the

Caumont sector west to the coast, with the River Vire being the boundary. The US First Army intelligence had, in fact, reported that there were no less than 12 divisions under these two corps that included the 17th SS Panzergrenadier and the 2nd SS Panzer Division *Das Reich*. Only the 2nd SS Panzer was reportedly below strength, both as a result of the battle of attrition since D-Day, the constant drain on manpower for replacement draft units, and the Allied air interdiction effort which prevented rapid battlefield reinforcement. As for the battle groups, only the elements from the 265th, 266th and 275th were available as mobile reserves. Despite the drain on manpower, German forces included several crack units, such as the 2nd Parachute and the two SS divisions.

The German position was further strengthened by the fact that the Seventh Army had bought itself precious time in delaying the American advance. This in turn gave Seventh Army units ample opportunity to prepare the ground thoroughly for a defensive battle. Likewise, whereas the First Army had very little room to manoeuvre offensively, the Seventh Army had plenty of room to manoeuvre, as well as an excellent line of communications necessary for maintaining a flexible defence.

Still, the Germans' greatest advantage lay in the terrain itself. The hedgerows which crisscrossed the entire area not only hampered offensive manoeuvre but limited the use of tanks. In fact, in an 12.8km (eight-mile) section of Normandy it was estimated by First Army intelligence that there

■ *Left:* **Men of the 79th Division around Lessay – mid-July. The rifle grenade was simple to use, being blown from the barrel by a blank cartridge.**

were over 3900 hedged enclosures. Growing out of the massive embankments that formed dikes up to 3m (10 feet) high, often flanked by drainage ditches or sunken roads, the hedges lent themselves easily to skilful organization of dug-in emplacements and concealed strongpoints. Besides the terrain, the dreary weather combined to accentuate the impact of the marshy terrain south and southwest of Carentan, which had been partially flooded months before by the Germans as a feature of their defence plans. The poor weather also negated the American advantage in airpower as more and more air strikes had to be cancelled, as were observation missions which restricted intelligence on enemy movements and dispositions.[7]

■ *Below:* The German 88mm *Panzerbusche* rocket-propelled AT weapon was an improved copy of the American bazooka design.

On 4 July, VII Corps went over to the attack with the 83rd Division fighting its first battle alongside the 90th Division of VIII Corps. The 83rd advanced along the Prairies Marécageuses, and reached Gorges to the west of the swamps and Sainteny to the east. The 4th Division was to attack through them towards Périers, followed by the 3rd Armored and 9th Divisions respectively. Unfortunately for the 83rd, the Germans had organized an extensive defence-in-depth and were ready with the strongest defensive effort in VII Corps' area.

Costly Attacks

During its first attack the 83rd lost 300 men, and made only slight gains over the following days. To bolster the 83rd's attack, General Collins threw in the 4th Division along a front mainly west of the Carentan-Périers highway. The soldiers of the 4th Division met the same determined enemy resistance as they attacked through no less than three main lines of resistance. After three days of heavy fighting, the 83rd and 4th Infantry Divisions had moved the front line only about 1828m (2000 yards) down the Carentan-Périers road.

Meanwhile, XIX Corps had initiated its battle with a push towards the River Vire with its ultimate objective being the high ground east and west of St-Lô. The town's importance centred on the fact that it served as a "hub" of roads connecting it with Carentan and Isigny; eastwards, roads suitable for heavy traffic leading towards Caumont and Bayeux; and to the west between Périers and Lessay the roads constituted the principal lines of communication behind the German west wing; while southwest lay the Coutances highway. By holding St-Lô, the Germans could reinforce their armies in the field in either direction. Thus, to deny the Germans this vital road junction was the

foremost thought of General Bradley and his staff.

There was one more advantage of taking St-Lô: its surrounding terrain was ideal for the breakout envisaged by SHAEF planners. The ground on both sides of St-Lô was ideal for launching an armoured offensive since it allowed the Americans to use their advantage in tanks which could operate much better than they had been doing in the *bocage*. If XIX Corps could get astride the River Vire or southwest towards Coutances, this would also present the Germans with another dilemma as to where to situate their defences.

Corlett's Plans

At the start of XIX Corps' drive, its left wing extended south in a considerable salient, flanked by the River Vire. Major-General Charles H. Corlett, XIX Corps commander, aimed his primary blow towards the west of the Vire, to gain ground which would bring that wing up on line. An advance here by XIX Corps would support the attack of VII Corps to the west, cover the flank of his own units on the right of the Vire, and pave the way for a direct attack on St-Lô east of the river. He planned to clear the enemy from the corps' zone west of the Vire as far as the high ground directly west of St-Lô, on which ran the highways towards Périers and Coutances. These roads were the final objective in his opening attack. While the 30th Division, supported by the 113th Cavalry Group, made this attack, the 29th Division (Brigadier-General Cota) would hold the ground east of the Vire, ready to attack on corps' order directly at St-Lô. The 35th Division, once it arrived in France and had been acclimatized to the area, was to join XIX Corps for the drive on St-Lô.

German forces facing XIX Corps belonged to both LXXXIV and II

Parachute Corps. The majority of German units had been formed in battle groups, but also included some crack infantry regiments. Total enemy strength was estimated to consist of 10 infantry, three engineer and two parachute battalions plus two companies of armour. West of the Vire, the sector facing XIX Corps' opening attack was part of the 32km (20-mile) front held by the 17th SS Panzergrenadier Division. Its right wing consisted of Battle Group *Heintz*, which included two rifle battalions of the 275th Division, the 275th Engineer Battalion, and the Engineer Battalion *Angers*; its artillery consisted of one battery from a regiment that was once a part of the 352nd Division, and one antiaircraft battery. West of St Jean-de-Daye, elements of the 38th SS Armoured Infantry Regiment faced XIX Corps' attack zone. The bulk of the 17th SS Panzergrenadier Division was already committed against US VII Corps.[8]

The Attack Towards St-Lô

The 30th Division (XIX Corps), commanded by Major-General Leland S. Hobbs, was to open the attack for St-Lô. The immediate objective of the 30th Division was the area of St-Jean-de-Daye, including the important crossroads just south of that village and the small elevation to the east. The 30th Division's plan called for a two-pronged assault which entailed crossing both the Vire and the adjoining Vire-Taute Canal; the 117th Infantry Regiment was to spearhead the assault on the Vire at 04:30 hours on the morning of 7 July, while the 120th Infantry Regiment was to attack the canal at 13:45 hours. The 119th Infantry, with the exception of one battalion guarding the flank along the east bank of the Vire from Aire to la Meauffe, was to support the Vire crossing and then follow the route of the 117th Infantry.

Leading the attack of the 117th Infantry was the 2nd Battalion, commanded by Lieutenant-Colonel Arthur H. Fuller, which was to commence the crossing with two rifle companies attacking abreast. Company G was to support the left and cross at a 10-minute interval after Company F. Engineer guides and 16 assault boats were provided by the 105th Combat Engineer Battalion for each of the leading companies. Each boat had been equipped with grappling hooks mounted on scaling ladders designed specifically by the engineers as a means of getting from the river up the steep banks, which were about 2.4m (eight feet) high on both sides of the Vire.

After assembling near the river behind a series of hedgerows, Fuller's 2nd Battalion awaited the commencement of an artillery barrage aimed against suspected German positions. While the bombardment went forward the soldiers of the 117th ran to their assigned boats, boarded them and proceeded across the river. With each boatload carrying 12 men, each of the troops reached the far shore at 04:30 hours. While disembarking and heading for cover, the troops shortly came under heavy German artillery fire.

As more and more troops disembarked German fire intensified considerably. Almost as soon as the soldiers proceeded from the banks of the river inland across an open field, German machine-gun and rifle fire opened up against them from the first row of hedgerows. In one instance, one platoon from Company F, 2nd Battalion, after breaking across the open field and making it to the first line of hedgerows, had gone too far off its mark and shortly encountered a small force of Germans, whereupon a stiff firefight commenced. This was the case throughout Company F's sector, as

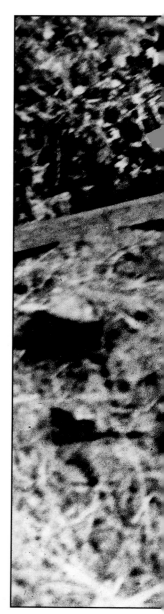

■ *Above:*
Fallschirmjaeger
**defences around
St-Lô. The foxhole
is behind and
below the facing
hedge and is safe
from just about
everything but
accurate plunging
fire.**

more hedgerows came alive with German troops firing at the Americans scrambling for cover. Despite the German resistance, the 2nd Battalion had secured its first objective by 08:30 hours that morning.

Before noon all three battalions of the 117th Infantry were across the Vire, followed by the 2nd Battalion of the 119th Infantry, with the advancing front being progressively enlarged as the attack developed. The 3rd Battalion, 117th Infantry, began pushing towards Hill 30, the high ground 1371m (1500 yards) east of St-Jean-de-Daye. The 1st Battalion advanced southwest and followed the 2nd Battalion which had been moving progressively along the Aire road towards the crossroads below St-Jean-de-Daye, attacking in squad columns through the open fields between the hedgerows. By noon, the battalion had reached its initial objectives. German resistance had been

relatively light, and in fact by noon of the 7th their defending units had been forced to withdraw.

As the 117th widened its bridgehead, the 120th prepared to attack the Vire-Taute Canal at 13:45 hours on the afternoon of the 7th. It had been hoped that the attack could be timed so as to unhinge the German defences facing the 117th and thereby force the enemy to withdraw. After meeting initial resistance, the 120th established its bridgehead and advanced astride the Pont-Hebert road with a company of M-4 Shermans.

By 16:00 hours both regiments were across the Vire and the Vire-Taute Canal respectively. As the regiments dug in a terrific artillery duel commenced between the Germans and the

■ *Above:* The Normandy battlefield was strewn with the rotting carcasses of cattle killed in the fighting Despite the smell, they made useful cover!

144

Americans. Both the 2nd Battalion, 117th Infantry, and the 2nd Battalion, 119th Infantry, attempted to continue the advance south towards St-Fromond-Eglise, though they met considerable enemy artillery fire from the deadly 88mm guns that pounded the route of their advance. Despite the slight pause in the advance that occurred later that day, it became apparent to all that the 30th Division had quickly learned the lessons of fighting in the *bocage*. The army's official history of the St-Lô campaign stated that the 30th's experience was typical of infantry divisions entering France after June 1944:

"In general, attacking units were finding what every division learned the hard way in its opening battles in Normandy: that hedgerow terrain demanded tactical skill and know-how which green units – and even those experienced in African or Sicilian fighting – did not initially possess. The 30th Division was no exception. Coming into Normandy in mid-June, the division had plenty of warning of trouble, and had trained to meet it. But there was no substitute for battle experience to bring out the concrete difficulties of action or test the methods for meeting them. Enemy fire positions were hard to locate and the harder to attack in a way that used full firepower of the ground units; artillery support was not easy to coordinate; communications within attacking forces larger than a platoon could be completely lost in the maze of hedgerows after a short advance; armour had to work blindly at ranges which meant dangerous exposure to bazookas and antitank guns; coordinated attacks were exceedingly difficult to manage, and a high premium was put on the individual leadership of a small unit.

"All this took time to learn and more time to digest; most units in the July battle were training as they fought."[9]

Despite the initial problems the 30th Division encountered as it entered battle, it had made one of the best advances in the First Army's month-long battle in the hedgerows. In fact, the 30th Division made such good progress that General Bradley was becoming more optimistic of the possibility of a local breakthrough occurring in the 30th Division's zone. Accordingly, General Bradley ordered Major-General Leroy H. Watson's 3rd Armored Division to be prepared to make a power drive through the bridgehead and onto the high ground southwest of St-Lô. General Bradley and his intelligence officers believed that the German resistance in 3rd Armored's area was minimal at best and that General Watson's force would have no trouble in penetrating what token resistance he might meet. Major-General Leland S. Hobbs, commanding general of the 30th thereby ordered his regiments, particularly the 117th, to keep attacking.

The 113th Cavalry Group

Also waiting to exploit the impending breakthrough by the 30th Division was the 113th Cavalry Group which had been assigned to provide support to the 120th Infantry Regiment. The 113th Cavalry had crossed the Vire-Taute Canal by 20:30 hours on 7 July, and by 02:00 hours the following morning was firmly in position on the far bank, and shortly thereafter began mobile operations. Troop A, 113th Cavalry, soon initiated the advance, pushing southwest on the road towards Goucherie. By midnight of 7/8 July, it had reached the road junction 640m (700 yards) from Goucherie, where the advance was halted by an enemy strongpoint that consisted of a platoon or more of men armed with machine guns, machine pistols and antitank guns.

145

■ *Opposite:* The capture of Hauts-Vents on 11 July 1944.

■ *Below:* A *Fallschirmjaeger* member near St-Lô in early July 1944.

At 03:00 hours, Troop A, 113th Cavalry, along with the assistance of the 230th Field Artillery Battalion, launched a coordinated attack on Goucherie which it had captured by 07:30 hours that morning. As the other cavalry units attached to the 120th sought to manoeuvre around Goucherie, it was hit by heavy enemy fire 1.6km (one mile) west of the town. Here, the German 639th *Ostermark* Battalion and 38th SS Panzergrenadier Regiment put up stubborn resistance which temporarily halted the 113th's advance. Once again, American hopes had been dashed for a war of manoeuvre as the attack bogged down into a series of infantry firefights, in which the troopers in their M-5 light tanks and

M-8 armoured cars had to run a deadly gauntlet of German machine-gun, mortar, antitank and rifle fire positioned in the hedgerows that straddled the highway. At several points during the battle, the fighting became so severe and confused that many of the troopers had to fight dismounted from their vehicles, and were thus unable to use the advantage of firepower from the weapons on their tanks and armoured vehicles. Eventually, however, with the assistance of Troops B and C, the squadron overcame German resistance.

Meanwhile, General Bradley's plan for pushing the 3rd Armored Division into the zone of the 30th Division, in the hope of driving through to the south, was put into operation during

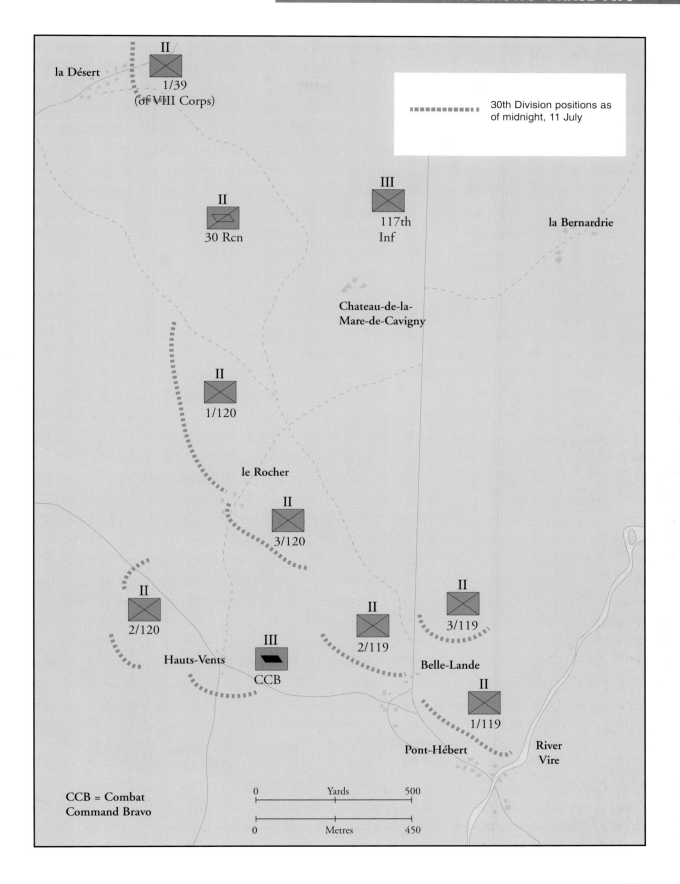

la Désert

II
1/39
(of VIII Corps)

30th Division positions as
of midnight, 11 July

II
30 Rcn

III
117th
Inf

la Bernardrie

Chateau-de-la-
Mare-de-Cavigny

II
1/120

le Rocher

II
3/120

II
3/119

II
2/119

II
2/120

Hauts-Vents

III
CCB

Belle-Lande

II
1/119

Pont-Hébert

River
Vire

CCB = Combat
Command Bravo

0   Yards   500

0   Metres   450

■ *Right:* The threat from the skies came from patrolling rocket-armed fighter-bombers such as the Republic P-47 (seen here), and the British Hawker Typhoon.

the night of 7/8 July. Major-General Watson's 3rd Armored Division was already on the move, and had been ordered by General Bradley to launch an immediate attack in the direction of St-Gilles, west of St-Lô. The first unit of the 3rd Armored Division to see action was Combat Command Bravo (CCB), commanded by Brigadier-General John J. Bohn.

Divided into three task forces (X, Y and Z), CCB began to move at 18:30 hours, and at 22:30 hours began crossing the bridge from Airel over the Vire at the rate of 45 vehicles an hour. Each task force was composed of a battalion of tanks, a battalion of armoured vehicles, a battalion of armoured infantry and a platoon of engineers. CCA (Combat Command A) remained in division reserve, being positioned at Ste-Marguerite d'Elle, ready to assist CCB if necessary. Shortly after crossing the Vire, CCB encountered small-arms fire about 548m (600 yards) from St-Fromond-Eglise. That night, as the 83rd Reconnaissance Battalion probed enemy lines, the Germans launched a powerful infantry-led counterattack consisting of mortars and artillery. Company D of the 83rd was forced to withdraw as the German bombardment continued into the early hours of the next day.

Meanwhile, General Watson ordered Brigadier-General Bohn to take CCB southwest from the St-Fromond area diagonally across the 30th Infantry Division's sector in order to stabilize the front. At 06:42 hours on 8 July, CCB began its attack southwest through hedgerow country, where it met a violent enemy counterattack from tanks

■ *Above:* July, on the attack south from Cherbourg, an M-4 Sherman and supporting infantry crawl towards the village of la Haye-du-Poits, north of Lessay.

that belonged to Battle Group *Heintz* (275th Fusilier Battalion). In the ensuing tank battle, four German Mk IVs were destroyed while CCB lost one tank. Thus, the armour of CCB became involved in the same tortuous hedgerow fighting that had been a constant feature of everyday life for the infantry in Normandy since D-Day.

The men and vehicles of Task Force X, meanwhile, moving southwest along the St-Fromond–Bordigny–la Bernardrie highway, encountered fierce enemy resistance from German machine guns and mortars dug in along the hedgerows, as well as from roving 88mm guns.

Without taking anything away from the tank crews of CCB, the most strident gains in this advance were actually made by the men of the 1st Battalion, 120th Infantry, and the 3rd Battalion, 117th Infantry, which

secured the crossroads south of the village of St-Jean-de-Daye.

The sense of frustration felt by the tankers of CCB was heightened by the massive congestion that occurred in the rear areas at Airel along the Vire, as the infantrymen bitterly complained about the congestion on the roads. Meanwhile, the tankers complained that the infantrymen were in their way and had pitched their tents in what had been designated as combat assembly areas. Eventually, the tankers of CCB and CCA were ordered by General Hobbs to travel by roads and avoid the fields, where German artillery had zeroed in on them. Apparently, General Hobbs believed that the combat command was not acting aggressively enough to get out of the hedgerow country. Eventually, however, General Bohn finally succeeded in reorganizing his task force to ensure that it could move in column along parallel routes without the delay of ploughing abreast through the fields. Nonetheless, CCB's continued delays brought General Hobbs to conclude that Brigadier-General Bohn lacked what it took to get CCB moving, and warned his subordinate that either he reach the objective or relinquish his command.

German Reserves

One reason for higher headquarters being insistent on getting CCB rolling was its knowledge of the approach of substantial enemy forces: from the west a part of the 2nd SS Panzer Division and a reinforced infantry battalion supported by a tank company; and from the east the full power of the Panzer *Lehr* Division. As General Corlett and his staff braced themselves for this onslaught of German armour, it became even more important that both CCB and CCA proceed on ahead towards their objective of Hauts-Vents.

Late in the morning of 9 July, small probing elements of a tank-infantry task force from the 2nd SS Panzer Division struck the 30th Division's right flank near le Desert, confirming General Corlett's and Hobbs' worst fears. By noon, however, the infantrymen of the 30th Division had contained this first German threat, though as events turned out it was only the prelude to a larger German effort. Almost as soon as the division's artillery had begun to redeploy, another German task force of infantry, tanks, artillery and self-propelled guns struck the 30th's right flank. Despite the confusion that existed during the early stages of the battle, divisional artillery once again came through as it pummelled the German advance with a massive barrage.

Tank Ambush

The victory was not without American casualties, however, as the Germans demonstrated they were not defeated. While pursuing two Mk IV tanks down a country road, a company from the 743rd Tank Battalion, which had been attached to the 30th Division, fell into a carefully laid ambush. German tanks, with sirens attached, attacked their pursuers from the flank at close range, and within 15 minutes the tank company had lost most of its equipment. Three M-4 Shermans had to be abandoned, while a further nine tanks and an engineer dozer tank had been destroyed in the mêlée. The company lost five soldiers killed, four wounded and 36 missing. Having lost two tanks the previous day to enemy fire, the company was virtually destroyed.[10]

With rumours of an impending German counterattack, and the destruction of the tank company of the 743rd to German armour, American infantrymen began withdrawing from their advanced positions. Eventually, CCB finally proceeded towards the St-

Jean-de-Daye-Pont Hebert highway, though the confusion continued as to the whereabouts of the Germans. Just as it appeared that Brigadier-General Bohn might reach his objective, General Hobbs called a halt in order to reorganize his infantry for the final lunge towards Hauts-Vents.

After more confusion as to CCB's location, it became apparent that the combat command was not at Hauts-Vents. In keeping with his threat of relief, General Hobbs relieved Brigadier-General Bohn of command of CCB. Eventually, however, a contingent of CCB did achieve its objective – Hill 91 – on the evening of 10 July, though an enemy artillery and mortar barrage then forced its withdrawal. Though unsuccessful in its initial attempts to hold Hill 91, CCB nonetheless disrupted Panzer *Lehr*'s preparations for attack that had been planned to start shortly after midnight. Combat Command B once again attacked towards Hill 91 on 11 July. Enemy guns east of the River Vire knocked out six tanks, though this time it did not prevent the tankers from continuing their advance. After being beaten back temporarily, Colonel Dorrance S. Roysdon, CCB's new commanding officer, personally led his men forward and finally secured Hauts-Vents.

Endless Delays

The entrance of CCB into the bridgehead had resulted in another frustrating round of hedgerow fighting and stalled advances. As was the case with the entire front of the First Army, CCB's initial failure to take its objective and exploit the breach caused a further delay in General Bradley's goal of a breakthrough towards St-Lô. Whereas the US Army's official history put some of the blame on what it called the combat command's inability to coordinate its activities with those of the

30th Infantry Division, the fact remains that CCB's inability to secure Hauts-Vents was due more to the appearance of Panzer *Lehr* and, more importantly, the confusion that had gripped the infantrymen of the 30th Division. Furthermore, the inability of the 39th Infantry Division to advance beyond le Desert in support of the 30th Division exposed the latter to possible counterattack by the Germans. In any analysis of this opening round to take St-Lô, it becomes clear that part of the problem lay with General Bradley's unrealistic expectations that a solitary reinforced tank battalion could exploit any breakthrough amidst two of the best German armoured divisions in Northwest Europe. In any event, the opportunity to make a deep penetration had been missed, for by the time CCB had untangled itself from the congestion with the 30th Division along the Vire, Panzer Lehr and elements of the 2nd SS Panzer Division had plugged the gap and were themselves preparing to counterattack.

The German Counterattack

Up to now, the German effort in the *bocage* country was to halt the First Army's rapid advance inland. Even as June turned to July, and a new commanding general took control of German forces in the West, the argument concerning how best to contain the Allied forces from pushing inland raged inside OKW and OB West.

As late as June 1944 it became apparent to all that the mobile strategy as advocated by the former Commander-in-Chief of OB West, Field Marshal von Rundstedt, had been the correct strategy in dealing with the Allied armies. Unfortunately, as every day passed, both the Americans and British forces became stronger, as

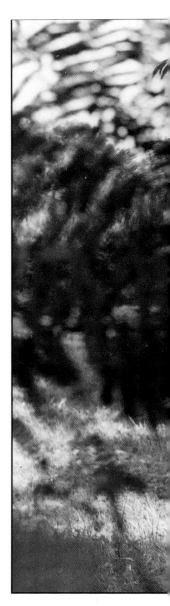

illustrated by the arrival of the 9th Infantry Division on the flank of the US XIX Corps. Panzer *Lehr*'s counterattack on 11 July caused problems in the 9th Division's lines, where the main strength of the enemy's attack fell, than it did farther south and east. The initial success of the German armour was due to a gap that had developed between the 39th and 47th Infantry Divisions.

Beginning at midnight, the 39th Infantry reported heavy German movement southwest of le Desert. In the early hours of 11 July Panzer *Lehr* struck. Within an hour, enemy armour and infantry columns began pouring into the gap between the 39th and 47th Infantry Divisions. One column from Panzer *Lehr* overran the command post of the 3rd Battalion, 47th Infantry, while another enemy formation pushed the 1st Battalion, 39th Infantry, back 548m (600 yards) along the la Desert highway. In fact, the impetus of the enemy attack carried some German armoured elements forward as much as

■ *Above:* Racing between hedgerows around Mortain, men of Collins' VII Corps are caught in the midst of the German Seventh Army counterattack, which began on 7 August.

1828m (2000 yards) behind the First Army's frontline positions.

The enemy counterattack destroyed the lines of communication between the 39th and 47th Infantry Regiments and division headquarters. While the 1st Battalion, 39th Infantry, withdrew, division headquarters took prompt action in order to "plug the gap" and prevent a German breakthrough. Even as reinforcements rushed to contain the enemy attack, the 899th Tank Destroyer Battalion and other units of the 39th and 47th Infantry Regiments fought it out with Panzer *Lehr*. Meanwhile, the 1st Battalion, 47th Infantry and four M-10 tank destroyers were directed by division headquarters to move down the road south of le Mesnil-Veneron; the mission of this force was to contact the 3rd Battalion, 47th Infantry, cut the enemy escape route and mop up isolated pockets of enemy resistance within the regimental area. The 3rd Battalion, 39th Infantry, was sent to block the German infantry from advancing in the la Scellerie-la Buhotrie area. Meanwhile, P-47 Thunderbolt aircraft flew several close air support sorties against German tanks moving along the road near le Desert in the vicinity of la Scellerie. At 12:30 hours, the 2nd Battalion, 60th Infantry, was brought forward to support the 47th Infantry Regiment. Eventually, the 3rd Battalion, 47th Infantry, was able to recover its command post fully intact.

The heaviest fighting of the day occurred in the sectors held by Companies A and B, 899th Tank Destroyer Battalion, which had been already alerted and were standing ready

■ *Below:* German infantry get a ride on a captured French Renault UE tractor, pressed into Wehrmacht service. The towed AT gun is a PAK 35/36.

to meet the German attack. Upon contact with the advancing German infantry, the American tankers beat back three attempts by the enemy to penetrate their lines between 03:00 hours and 06:00 hours. Before daylight, a platoon of M-10 tank destroyers belonging to Company A attached to the 30th Infantry Division attacked three German tanks that had successfully penetrated about 457m (500 yards) into the American lines. During the tank-versus-tank destroyer duel that followed, the Americans managed to destroy one German tank while they themselves lost one M-10 tank destroyer. The other two German tanks, which had also been hit and had spouted flames, fled back to their own lines.

Panzer *Lehr* was not, however, finished with the attack. To the west of le Desert, approximately 10 German tanks (primarily Mk IVs and Mk V Panthers) drove north on an unimproved road that led from the crossroads at le Hommet-d-Arthenay to la Charlemerie, and succeeded in reaching a point just south of la Scellerie. Here the column was stopped when elements of the 3rd Platoon, Company A, managed to destroy the leading German tank while losing one of its M-10s. With the arrival of infantry reinforcements and in order to deal more effectively with the German attack, Company A's commanding officer reorganized his force into an effective tank-infantry team which

■ *Above:* US infantry make a dash into the main street of the village of St-Ensy. From the wrecked buildings, it seems that the German garrison has already undergone a heavy Allied bombardment.

■ *Above:* During the Normandy campaign the Allies had in theatre over 3700 fighters and fighter-bombers, including these P-51 Mustangs.

managed to destroy three German Mk Vs and a halftrack before the remainder of the German force withdrew under heavy fire.

Even as the tank crews and infantrymen of Company A were duelling with the German tanks, Company C, 899th Tank Destroyer Battalion, had enjoyed its first actions against a well-camouflaged Mk V

Panther tank moving along a road near le Chalemenerie by taking a page out of the German hedgerow tactics manual. As the unsuspecting German tank rounded a bend in the road, an M-10 greeted it with two rapid shots from its 3in main armament, knocking the Panther out and killing two of its crew, and scattering the accompanying infantrymen.

This action was repeated in the early afternoon as several of Company C's M-10 tank destroyers opened up on a Mk V Panther. In the brief but violent duel that followed, two M-10s "jumped" a Panther which managed to disable one M-10 and kill three of its crew. Meanwhile the German tank, which had also been damaged, was then picked off by another M-10 which fired two shots point-blank into the crippled German tank. In another engagement, an M-10 managed to disable another Mk V whose crew abandoned her as she slid off the road and into a hedgerow embankment along the road. This scene went on all afternoon as the infantrymen of the 1st Battalion, 47th Infantry, continued to pick off the German tanks.

Allied Air Attack

Even as tank battalions such as the 899th Tank Destroyer Battalion and infantry teams armed with bazookas duelled with the German soldiers of Panzer *Lehr*, it became quite apparent by 16:00 hours that the American lines would hold. Together with P-47 Thunderbolts and P-51 Mustangs flying close air support missions, the infantrymen of the 9th Division managed to turn back this latest, and possibly most serious, of all German counterattacks in front of St-Lô. In sum, the defeat of Panzer *Lehr*'s counterattack was the best example of a combined effort between the infantry and armour, and armour and air power. In one engagement alone, the P-47s and P-51s managed to destroy 13 out of 14 tanks situated near le Hommet-de-Arthenay. In fact, as the official US Army history states:

"Joint efforts of air and ground forces had neutralized the Panzer *Lehr* Division breakthrough by 16:00. The 39th and 47th Infantry Regiments were then ordered to advance and reoccupy their positions of the morning. By 21:00 their mission was completed against light opposition, and the regiments were instructed to dig in for the night in preparation for an attack the following day. The net effect of the German counterattack had thus been little more than to cause a day's loss in the 9th Division's schedule of advance."[11]

After throwing back the German attack, the 30th Division managed to continue its advance at least in one sector even while beating back scattered German breakthroughs along its front.

Despite the German attack, the US 79th Infantry Division managed to enter La Haye-du-Puits on 7 July while the 8th Division took over the centre of VII Corps' front. The 90th Division, meanwhile, met determined German resistance in the Monte-Castre Forest sector but was able to fight its way through the terrain, as well as the German defenders. On the corps' right flank, the 79th Division became wrapped up once again in the hedgerows as the German defenders managed to limit the division's advance to a mere 182m (200 yards). Finally, by 10 July, all three divisions began to move forward against an enemy that was now well and truly on the defensive. By then end of 11 July, VIII Corps had managed to push about 2743m (3000 yards) beyond La Haye-du-Puits. More importantly, combined with the failure of Panzer *Lehr*'s attack, it was now apparent to Generals Bradley and Corlett that the enemy's main line of resistance had finally been breached.

Despite the fact that the fighting had resulted in a casualty figure that exceeded 5000 men, with each attacking division sustaining the loss of several hundred casualties per day, it was apparent to General Bradley that there was positive movement towards the St-Lô objective. VII Corps' efforts met equally determined German resistance, though it must be stated that by 10 July the German lines had shown signs of wear and tear. What spared VII Corps was the arrival of the 9th Infantry Division, and its ability immediately to jump into action on 11 July against the determined German attack by the Panzer *Lehr* Division.

Summary

A week of heavy fighting, however, had resulted in a further delay in General Bradley's desire to seize St-Lô, and thereby position himself for the much anticipated breakout. In fact, American soldiers were in little position to feel anything save disappointment over the results of a bitter struggle for a few miles of ground. General Bradley's desire to avoid a battle of stalemate had been barely avoided: the 30th and 9th Divisions offered some hope of a breakthrough in their actions at Hauts-Vents and La Haye-du-Puits. Yet, as General Bradley noted:

"By July 10, we faced a real danger of a World War I-type stalemate in Normandy. Montgomery's forces had taken the northern outskirts of Caen, but the city was not by any means in his control. The airfield sites still lay beyond his grasp. My own breakout had failed. Despite enormous casualties and loss of equipment, the Germans were slavishly following Hitler's orders to hold every yard of ground. We, too, had suffered heavy casualties; about 22,000 in the British sector; over 30,000 in the American sector."[12]

The failure of the First Army to push beyond la Haye-du-Puits and Hauts-Vents can be attributed to many factors:

logistical, manpower, inter-Allied squabbling and poor weather. The real reason, however, lay in the fact that the German decision to contest every yard of ground forced the First Army to fight a war of attrition, something that Overlord planners overlooked or simply neglected in the invasion plan's original conception. Despite the mixed quality of the German troops in the Normandy

■ *Above:* A US bazooka team covers a road in the Forest of Ardaine in July 1944.

sector, it can be said with some degree of accuracy that Hitler's stand-fast order had its intended effect, with the result that the upcoming fight for St-Lô would resemble the same type of bitter attritional fighting that had already taken place in the hedgerows and fields before it.

In spite of the setbacks and slow approach towards St-Lô, General Bradley began to prepare for his breakout from the Cotentin Peninsula. Part of the plan involved attacking along a narrow front spearheaded by Major-General Collins' VII Corps, with its first objective being the seizure of St-Lô and its important road junction. In this way, the stage was set for the last major battle of the bloody *bocage* country of Normandy.

159

CHAPTER V:

THE BATTLE WON

The capture of St-Lô, and the end of *bocage* fighting. The eve of Operation Cobra and the breakout into France, 12–20 July.

Throughout the month of June the US First Army had clawed its way to within the very outskirts of the vital town of St-Lô. Here, the tenacious, almost fanatical German resistance had reluctantly given ground to the material weight of the American forces under Lieutenant-General Omar Bradley. As Field Marshal Montgomery's Twenty-First Army Group battled the élite formations of the Waffen-SS and hardened Wehrmacht units for Caen, General Bradley prepared a narrow-fronted offensive designed to "unhinge" the German left flank. The main effort of this renewed offensive by the First Army was to be carried out by the 29th Division, aimed at the ridges straddling the St-Lô-Bayeux highway, and then St-Lô itself. On its right flank, the US 35th Division was to exert pressure between the River Vire and the Isigny-St-Lô highway, its objective being the right bank of the Vire. As the 35th Division carried through its portion of the attack, the 30th Division was to advance along the other side of the Vire. On the 29th Division's left flank, an assault against Hill 192 would be made by the 2nd Division of V Corps. The capture of Hill 192 was important as it would serve as the main artillery observation point for the assault on St-Lô itself.

■ *Left:* On 18 July St-Lô finally fell to the First Army. Infantry and armour (from the 2nd or 29th Divisions) enter the town with care from the north down the Isigny-St-Lô road. The main line of attack to take the town, however, had been from the east.

General Bradley's Field Order to VII, VIII and XIX Corps had provided for the extension eastwards of their offensive, with the last stage to be a coordinated attack by three divisions through hills protecting St-Lô. First scheduled for 9 July, the attack east of the Vire had been postponed due to heavy enemy resistance and Panzer *Lehr*'s armoured thrust at General Corlett's XIX Corps' right flank. While the American commanders did not realize it at the time the failure of Panzer *Lehr* to break through the American lines was the last desperate attempt of Field Marshal Rommel's Seventh Army to reverse the situation in Normandy. Failure meant that the Allied buildup on the Normandy beaches would continue, with more and more combat units and materiel being put ashore.

German Defences

German forces in and around St-Lô, however, remained very formidable. First Army G-2 (Intelligence) had identified most of II Parachute Corps, including two regiments of the 3rd Parachute Division, elements of four infantry regiments and a weak remnant of the 352nd Division. The parachute regiments were among the more troubling, as they consisted of crack troops who had helped to halt V Corps in its initial breakout from the Omaha beachhead, and had subsequently defended Hill 192 against every attack to date. The German infantry units were organized into battle groups that averaged anywhere from 400 to 500 men from as many as three separate divisions. One group of infantrymen, for example, was made up of elements from three battalions of the 353rd Division (the main units of which were fighting in the battle around Monte-Castre); a second battle group was built around three battalions of the 266th Division; and the

group comprising the remnants of the 352nd Division was estimated on 7 July to have only 800 men. Both the paratroopers and infantrymen had artillery support from 24 105mm howitzers, 12 150mm howitzers, one battery of 150mm *Nebelwerfers* and two batteries of the feared dual-purpose 88mm guns. II Parachute Corps, for all its infantry prowess, had no known armoured support.[1]

Even as Panzer *Lehr*'s tanks struck the American lines, several small German attacks were launched in order to straighten the lines of the Wehrmacht defences. These were not as severe, however, as Panzer *Lehr*'s major attack beyond the Vire. One of these German attacks was aimed at the 1st Battalion, 115th Infantry, by the 1st Battalion, 9th Parachute Regiment, which, under a hail of mortar and artillery fire, quickly overran the 115th's forward outposts. The 1st Battalion was holding a broad front with all three companies in line, with the German attack coming between both A and B Companies. Initially, the *Fallschirmjaeger* managed to cut off and destroy two platoons as both infantry companies desperately fought to avoid an enemy breakthrough. Survivors of the battle remembered that NCOs and officers, gunners and privates fought in small groups to win battle.

By 07:30 hours, the Germans had given up and had retired from the battlefield, leaving their dead behind. In the attack, both the 115th Infantry Regiment and the German paratroopers lost approximately 100 men each. A similar attack was made by elements of the German 5th Parachute Regiment against the soldiers of the 2nd Division. While it caused some consternation early on, the *Fallschirmjaeger* assault failed to disrupt the 2nd Division's scheduled attack on Hill 192.

■ *Right:* An MG42 team of panzer-grenadiers guards a major road junction. They are supported by a tank across the road behind them. Their machine gun is on a tripod mount for sustained firing.

■ *Above:* A German StuG IV assault gun receives fresh ammunition for its main 75mm armament from members of the *Munitionstaffel*, the ammunition echelon of the battalion's supply company.

General Bradley's plan for the seizure of St-Lô began with moves to secure the surrounding high ground in order that the artillery could have unobstructed observation when it began laying down fire support for the attacking divisions. Part of the task of securing the high ground had been assigned to the 29th Infantry Division, commanded by Major-General Charles H. Gerhardt, and the 2nd Infantry Division, commanded by Major-General Walter M. Roberts. While the 29th protected its left flank, soldiers of the 2nd Division were to attack Hill 192.

The 2nd Division was, as the US Army's official account of the battle stated, "considered a good unit", and its commanding general had no illusion as to the problems he faced in getting to the top, as his forces had attempted a similar feat in June before being thrown off by heavy German resistance. Prior to this second assault, however, the soldiers of the 2nd and 29th Divisions had a month of hedgerow fighting under their belts, and had become battle-wise as to what lay ahead. During the period 16 June to 11 July, the 2nd Division had practised the taking of Hill 192, and thus were well aware of the need for intensive training in infantry-tank tactics, as well as the need for accurate artillery and air support. In fact, in the case of the artillery, fire plans were based on numbered grid squares measuring

91m (100 yards) each side, which had been designed to ensure proper infantry-artillery coordination during the assault. As for dealing with the hedgerows:

"A tank-infantry engineer team was devised for dealing with the hedgerow representing a new line of departure. When the engineers had blown a hole for the tanks to pass through, the tanks would enter the field, fire their 75mm guns into the corners, and spray the lateral hedgerow ahead to cover the infantry scouts advancing (in this case) along the axial hedges.

"These scouts would also be covered by BAR men. Two of the four demolitions men followed behind, and the engineers and the leader of the infantry squad would choose the best place for the tank to go through the next barrier. Special EE-8 phones were installed on the rear of the tanks and connected with the tank's interphone system for tank-infantrymen communications during action. Two engineers would stay with the vehicle to protect it during the advance, scanning and firing at side hedgerows to keep down the enemy bazooka teams. In the area close to the line of departure, hedgerow embankments were carefully scooped out on the American side, leaving a shell which the tanks could push through on the day of the attack." [2]

In order to employ best these newly developed tactics, Major-General

■ *Above:* A corpsman of the 82nd Airborne tends a German casualty around Ste Mere Eglise – one of the first villages to be liberated. German casualties rose dramatically through the summer, reaching an estimated 500,000 by September 1944.

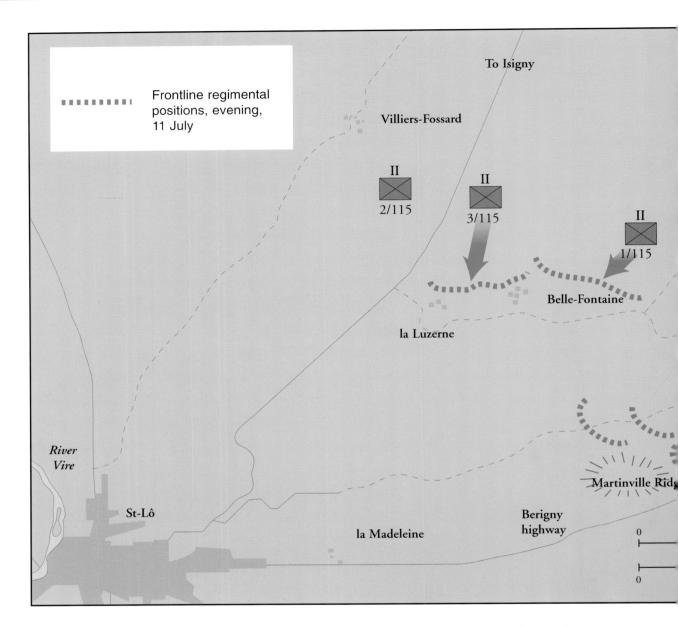

Frontline regimental positions, evening, 11 July

To Isigny

Villiers-Fossard

II
2/115

II
3/115

II
1/115

Belle-Fontaine

la Luzerne

River Vire

Martinville Ridge

St-Lô

la Madeleine

Berigny highway

0

0

■ *Above:* General Gerhardt's plan to flank St-Lô from the east. Despite German counterattacks on the 115th Infantry, by 12 July the 116th Infantry was on the high ground of Martinville Ridge.

Roberts ordered the division to conduct training specifically designed for the forthcoming assault:

"[This training emphasized] tank-infantry-engineer proficiency in applying the tactics of demolition, fire power, and speed in hedgerow terrain. To achieve speed in the attack, troops scooped holes, large enough for tanks to drive through, in the hedgerow embankments that served as the line-of-departure-holes that left a thin shell of

earth on the side facing the enemy; when the attack came, the tanks would be able to crash through under their own power. Bursting through the hollowed-out hedgerows, the tankers hoped to be upon the Germans in the next row before antitank weapons could be brought to bear."[3]

The 38th Infantry Regiment, commanded by Colonel Ralph W. Zwicker, was assigned to make the main assault with three tank companies and

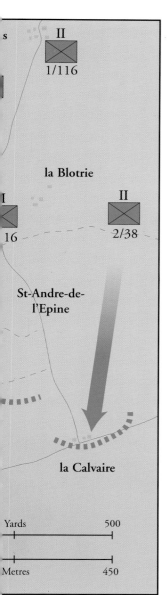

II
1/116

la Blotrie

I   II

16   2/38

St-Andre-de-
l'Epine

la Calvaire

Yards   500

Metres   450

two heavy mortar companies attached. Supporting the 38th was one battalion from the 23rd Infantry (Lieutenant-Colonel Jay B. Loveless), which was to send one battalion across the eastern slope of the objective. The 9th Infantry, led by Colonel Chester J. Hirschfelder, had been assigned the role of providing supporting fire for the division as it attacked. In addition to close air support from the Army Air Force's tactical wings, the division would have artillery and supporting tank support.

Heavy Resistance

Even as the attack jumped off, the soldiers belonging to the 38th Infantry met a heavy volume of fire that temporarily at least prevented them from reaching their line of departure. Part of this was due to the fact that the Germans had anticipated the length of the American pre-assault artillery bombardment and had withdrawn slightly until it was over, after which they reoccupied their positions in anticipation of the forthcoming attack. Here, the Germans brought up *Panzerfausts* with which they were able to stop the six tanks accompanying the 38th Infantry. This forced the infantry to drop their planned "scooping out" of the hedgerows and conduct a costly frontal assault. Nonetheless, with dogged determination the American infantrymen advanced steadily, though slowly, up the slopes of Hill 192 largely with the assistance of heavy artillery which fired 20,000 rounds, or 45.5 tonnes (45 tons), of high explosive against the objective. Other tanks and bazooka teams knocked out assault guns concealed in the rubble of a village adjoining Hill 192. A dozen riflemen from the 38th Infantry attacked a position referred to as "Kraut Corner", which was heavily reinforced with an antitank gun and *Fallschirmjaegers*. In

the ensuing battle, 15 enemy paratroopers surrendered while three others who refused were buried alive by a tank dozer.

As General Robertson reported to First Army Headquarters: "We have a battle on our hands . . . [but] . . . things are breaking a little a hundred yards here and a hundred yards there."[4] Despite the strong, often suicidal resistance offered by the German defenders, soldiers from the 38th Infantry were on the top of Hill 192 by noon of that day. Shortly thereafter, the Germans broke contact and withdrew, offering only minimal resistance to the American advance which now began the descent onto the southern slope. Part of the 38th Infantry dug in on a defensive perimeter just short of the highway and covered the road with rifle and automatic fire. Other elements of the regiment filtered across the road in small assault groups and organized the high ground immediately to the south.

Meanwhile, a battalion of the 23rd Infantry outflanked a gully nicknamed by the GIs as "Purple Heart Draw". Here, tanks fired on houses suspected of concealing German strongpoints. Several lucky shots by rifle grenades struck enemy held hedgerows at the right height to achieve the effect of air bursts over enemy crew-served weapons. By late afternoon, the battalion had crossed the east slope of Hill 192 and gained positions overlooking the Berigny highway.

That evening, not realizing that his forces had withdrawn from their positions on top of Hill 192, Colonel-General Hausser, the Seventh Army commander, ordered General of Paratroops Eugen Meindl, II Parachute Corps commander, to hold the position there at all costs. It was too late, for US artillery was now positioned on top of Hill 192 and firing with deadly effect onto the Berigny road. Despite several weak counterattacks, the Americans were on Hill 192 to stay. Nonetheless, the Germans began to establish new positions south of the Berigny highway.

On 12 July, the 2nd Division advanced very little as it consolidated its new positions atop Hill 192 and south of the Berigny road. As noted in the US Army's official history, the Germans, whose troops had been tied down by XIX Corps near St-Lô, "were relieved when the American attack halted . . . [for] . . . most German commanders felt that if the 2nd Division had continued its attack towards the south, the Americans would accomplished a clean breakthrough."[5] The 2nd Division's seizure of Hill 192 was the first major step towards taking St-Lô, though the cost was heavy. In two days of fighting, the division suffered 69 killed, 328 wounded and eight missing, though it captured the best observation point in the St-Lô sector, a point from which the Americans could look down the Martinville Ridge towards XIX Corps' objective.

Preliminary Plans for St-Lô
General Bradley's original scheme for taking St-Lô in early June involved an attack by XIX Corps east of the River Vire, followed by the main attacks in the Cotentin on 3 July by VIII Corps, and VII Corps on 4 July, with XIX's attempts to secure a bridgehead on the Vire on 7 July. German resistance, primarily stemming from the tortuous advance through hedgerow country and the lack of adequate reserves, forced General Bradley to extend his plan for the seizure of St-Lô, originally planned for 9 July, not once but twice within a 48-hour period. The First Army commander noted that given the nature of the opposition, as well as the strength of his own units, the seizure of St-Lô

would require at least two divisions attacking in unison, which could assist each other in depth.

With the arrival of the 35th Division, and the availability of the veteran 29th Division, Bradley believed he now possessed sufficient strength to take St-Lô. Located a mere 6.4km (four miles) from St-Lô, both the 29th and 35th Divisions held positions across an 12.8km (eight-mile) front that extended from la Meauffe through Villiers-Fossard to the Couvains-Calvaire road. St-Lô was directly in the centre of the XIX Corps' zone of operations. In order to secure St-Lô, the division would have to advance to the river line west of the town and to the Berigny road, the eastwards exit from the town.

The scheme of operation had both the 29th and 35th Divisions attacking abreast on a narrow front. The boundary that would separate the two attacks ran from Villiers-Fossard along the western base of Hill 122 to the loop of the Vire. The 35th on the right flank was to move to the 3.2km (two-mile) stretch of the Vire immediately northwest of St-Lô, while the 29th was to take the town itself. While one battalion of medium artillery was to support XIX Corps' attack west of the Vire, the remainder of the corps' artillery – four battalions of 155mm howitzers and a battalion each of 4.5in guns and 8in howitzers – was to assist the attack on St-Lô. In order to assure the capture of the town, General Corlett assigned an additional battalion of medium artillery to General Gerhardt's 29th Division.

Even while the 2nd Division was in the process of seizing Hill 192 and the adjoining Berigny highway, General Gerhardt's 29th Division and the newly arrived 35th Division prepared to assault the German positions on top of Martinville Ridge, another strategic

■ *Above:* July: US infantry storm one of the farmhouses dominating the roads to St-Lô.

position that would aid in the taking of St-Lô. The 29th Division, which had been fighting in Normandy since Omaha Beach on D-Day, was now made up primarily of veteran soldiers and had, in fact, participated in the first futile attempt to seize St-Lô in June. Having much experience in hedgerow fighting, General Gerhardt and his assistant division commander, Brigadier-General Norman

Cota, set out to prepare their troops for the task ahead.

For his part, General Gerhardt re-organized his forces into small tank-infantry-engineer teams and rehearsed their coordinated action according to a well-detailed and orchestrated plan that assigned an infantry squad and one tank to each hedgerowed field, and an engineer squad to each infantry platoon or three fields. He also directed the division ordnance company to weld iron prongs to his tanks so that they could ram holes in the hedgerow banks to facilitate the placing of demolition charges. General Cota also supervised a new tactical procedure whereby attention was paid to the necessity of training infantrymen to cross open centres of hedgerow-bordered fields, rather than moving along axial hedgerows. By training soldiers in this method of manoeuvre, General Cota had hoped that the GIs could avoid enfilading fire along the axial since in the past, squads and platoons had been too often pinned down by German automatic weapons which were normally set up at field corners.[6] Tanks were expected to provide whatever assistance they could in dealing with the hedgerows. Equipped with the iron prongs and "rhino" attachments, it now appeared that the GIs had an effective means of dealing with the German positions in the hedgerows.

The attack on Martinville Ridge commenced on 11 July. General Gerhardt's scheme of manoeuvre called for the main effort to be directed to the left or east. He thus deployed the 115th Infantry Regiment, commanded by Colonel Godwin Ordway, Jr., across a broad front, located north and northeast of Hill 122, on the division's right flank. Even though all three infantry battalions would attack abreast of each other, Gerhardt planned to make his main

effort the seizure of the Martinville Ridge. By holding the high ground east of St-Lô, US troops would then threaten the German positions atop Hill 122 with encirclement and isolation from the south. This would in turn force the enemy to withdraw from not only their hilltop positions but also St-Lô as well. This would allow American artillery to pummel the retreating German forces.

Below: On the road to St-Lô, a US motorized column comes to halt after enemy action up ahead. The danger is that this could be a prelude to a German ambush.

General Gerhardt now ordered the 116th Infantry Regiment, commanded by Colonel Charles D. W. Canham, to attack south along a narrow front near the division's left boundary to the Martinville Ridge. Once there, the regiment would wheel right and descend the ridge towards the eastern edge of the town. Meanwhile, the 115th Infantry was to launch a diversionary attack down the Isigny-St-Lô road towards Hill 122 and protect the division's right flank. The 175th Infantry, commanded by Colonel Ollie W. Reed, was to be prepared to exploit the success of these two regiments, either on the Martinville Ridge or from Hill 122.

Even as General Gerhardt's forces prepared to attack, XIX Corps' old

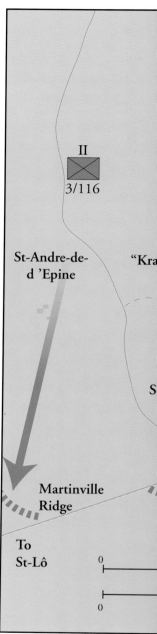

nemesis, II Parachute Corps and Panzer *Lehr*, launched a diversionary attack in the early hours of 11 July, aimed at a weak sector manned by a company sized unit of the 115th Infantry. For a while it appeared that the German attack, supported by two companies of *Fallschirmjaeger* and combat assault engineers might unhinge the American attack plan. As small groups of soldiers fought off the German assault, the latter for some unknown reason broke contact and withdrew to their former positions.

While the German attack was merely a raid, General Gerhardt believed that this possibly signalled the buildup of a major German counterattack that would enable them better to defend St-Lô. As for the raid itself, the 115th Infantry suffered over 100 casualties. More importantly, it disrupted their planned "jump off" for the attack on Martinville Ridge, which did not take place until later that afternoon. As anticipated, the soldiers of the 115th made little progress, impeded as they were by the hedgerows.

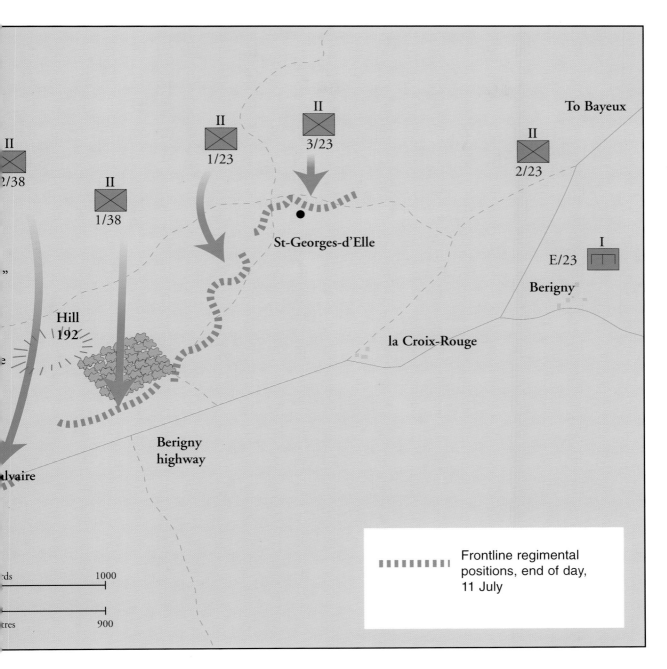

To Bayeux

II
1/23

II
3/23

II
2/23

II
1/38

II
2/38

St-Georges-d'Elle

I
E/23

Berigny

Hill
192

la Croix-Rouge

Berigny
highway

.lvaire

1000

900

rds

tres

▪▪▪▪▪▪▪▪▪ Frontline regimental
positions, end of day,
11 July

Meanwhile, General Gerhardt's attack commenced on schedule early that morning, when two battalions of the 116th Infantry jumped off in column formation behind a heavy artillery bombardment. Once again, determined German resistance, as well as the terrain, made the going slow. As the regiment's 4.2in mortars fired on the Martinville Ridge and tanks knocked out a German self-propelled gun on the la Calvaire road, the infantrymen reached their first major obstacle, a sunken road that was heavily mined and covered by automatic weapons.

Here, the advance slowed considerably as the fighting once again revolved around hedgerow after hedgerow. After nearly five hours of fighting, the regiment had secured only

■ *Above:* To the left of the 116th's move onto the Martinville Ridge, 38th Infantry took Hill 192 and cut the Berigny highway to the east.

173

■ *Above:* By 12 July the roads north and east of St-Lô had fallen to US troops. As the cordon tightened, German prisoners grew in number.

six hedgerows. Suddenly, German resistance collapsed as news of the 2nd Division's seizure of Hill 192 forced the enemy to beat a hasty retreat. The 116th Infantry then rapidly moved south to the Martinville Ridge, turned right and began to move down the ridge towards St-Lô. By the end of the day, the regiment's reserve battalion and a company of M-4 Sherman tanks had established a blocking position on the division's left flank, entrenched on the south slope of the Martinville Ridge. which overlooked the Berigny road that went into St-Lô. Victory was now within reach.

With the capture of Hill 192 and with positions on the Martinville Ridge, General Gerhardt's efforts to outflank Hill 122 from both the east and south promised success. The 2nd Division was now in position to move on St-Lô itself as well as cut off Hill 122. General Gerhardt alerted the 175th Infantry Regiment, his reserve unit, to conduct a passage of lines through the 116th on 12 July and drive towards the town from the east along the Berigny highway.

Heavy Artillery Fire

Unfortunately for the soldiers of the 116th Infantry, however, the terrain and the Germans would not cooperate, as the open fields, dotted by hedgerows and orchards, offered no protection as enfilading fire brought the advancing units under intense artillery shelling. In one instance, as the 29th Division pushed forward, it lost almost 500 men. In fact, throughout the battles on Hill 122 and Martinville Ridge, both the 2nd and 29th Divisions had to run a virtual gauntlet of German fire. Major-General Gerhardt's sole consolation was the fact that he occupied the southern slope of the Martinville Ridge, and thus could move along the Berigny highway into St-Lô. General Gerhardt and his staff concluded that he would have to take St-Lô by direct assault and occupy the town. On the evening of 11 July, he instructed Colonel Canham to push on, and if possible take St-Lô. The approaching darkness and well-entrenched German defenders proved to be his main impediments.

As for the German defences, while enemy commanders had been "unconcerned" about the tactical situation on the morning of 11 July, this had changed by noon of that day as American forces now occupied Hill 192 and Panzer *Lehr*'s attack had been beaten back. Likewise, German strength

in and around St-Lô had been drastically reduced as they clung tenaciously to their positions around the town. American artillery had been the primary culprit in the reduction of German strength. II Parachute Corps reported that its entire front had burst into flames, while the 3rd Parachute Regiment reported that its manpower levels had been reduced to 35 percent of their authorized strength. The battle group from the 352nd fighting alongside the *Fallschirmjaegers* had shrunk from 1000 to 180 men. Meanwhile, General Meindl had been rebuffed in his attempts to secure reserves from Brittany. In refusing Meindl's request, Colonel-General Hausser nevertheless insisted that the paratroops hold onto Martinville Ridge at all costs. General Meindl pointedly informed Hausser that, "someone was soon going to have to come up with a brilliant plan if they were to counter the American pressure."[7]

On 12 July, the 29th Infantry Division renewed the attack, making very little progress as German resistance stiffened. On the right flank, the 115th Infantry, which had been extended over a broad front without the benefit of a reserve, and under the watchful eyes of the Germans on Hill 122, did little more than maintain pressure and sustain casualties. On the left, the 175th Infantry was unable – because of German artillery fire – to pass through the 116th and position itself for the drive down the Martinville Ridge. German artillery and mortar fire immobilized the division and again inflicted heavy casualties.

Even as the 175th prepared to conduct its deployment, however, enemy fire began to deplete the 29th Division at an alarming rate. During the evening of 12 July, regimental commanders began to have serious doubts as to whether the attack would succeed, and they informed General Gerhardt that the general mood favoured taking up a strong defensive position to await an expected heavy enemy assault.

The 35th Division and Hill 122

In comparison to the veteran 2nd and 29th Divisions, the 35th Division was a relative newcomer to the struggle then going on in the hedgerows. Entering France on 5–7 July, the division moved from its assembly areas into its assigned sector east of the River Vire on 9–10 July. Commanded by Major-General Paul W. Baade, the 35th was by all accounts an extremely well-trained division. While sprinkled with veterans of the fighting in North Africa and Italy, as well as replacements, the division had been handicapped by its limited knowledge of the terrain it was about to fight over, and of the Germans' preparations in the 3.2km (two miles) of hedgerows which dominated the landscape that it would have to fight over to reach its objective on Hill 122.

General Baade's divisional attack was to commence at 06:00 hours on 11 July. Prior to the attack, German artillery pounded the 35th Division's jump-off positions near the Vire and along the entire divisional assembly area. The attack commenced on time, however, with two battalions of the 137th Infantry attacking abreast through murderous German fire. Immediately, Colonel Layng, the regimental commander, was wounded by a German machine-gun bullet. All along the front the American infantrymen met heavy machine-gun and mortar fire, reinforced by medium artillery and 88mm guns. After making initial progress, the attack began to bog down at St-Gilles as the 1st Battalion, 137th Infantry, ran into a labyrinth of German emplacements which included a fortified church in front of the town.

When the battalion came within 45m (50 yards) of the church and its cemetery, the Germans opened up with a heavy concentration of fire. Even with the commitment of the 3rd Battalion, 137th Infantry, and a pounding by division and corps artillery, the German position held. Farther east, the 2nd Battalion, 137th Infantry, met equally stiff resistance in front of the German main line of resistance (MLR). In fact, against the 2nd Battalion, the German employed tactics that had proven effective during the month of June in the hedgerow fighting. They tried to block the forward movement of advancing units along lateral hedgerows with fire from automatic weapons. Then, if they were successful in pinning the attacking American infantry down, they would call in artillery on top of them or waited for assault guns to appear while mortar fire blanketed the lateral hedgerows with a deadly bombardment.

Superior German Tactics

The 320th Infantry Regiment had a similar experience in its opening advance through hedgerow territory, particularly with respect to one of its rifle platoons. Here, a rifle platoon from Company E fell victim to German heavy mortars which had bracketed the area, with the result that all but 14 of its members were either killed or severely wounded. Enemy artillery fire also cut into communications and telephone wires which made communication all the more difficult, if not impossible, during the advance. This seriously affected the command and control of the attack.

On 12 July the 137th Infantry resumed the advance which had been stalled by stubborn German resistance. While the 1st Battalion had managed to "straighten out" its northern flank on

■ Right: The German garrison knew that the roads into St-Lô were vital to its defence and remorselessly targeted them with mortar, artillery and small-arms fire.

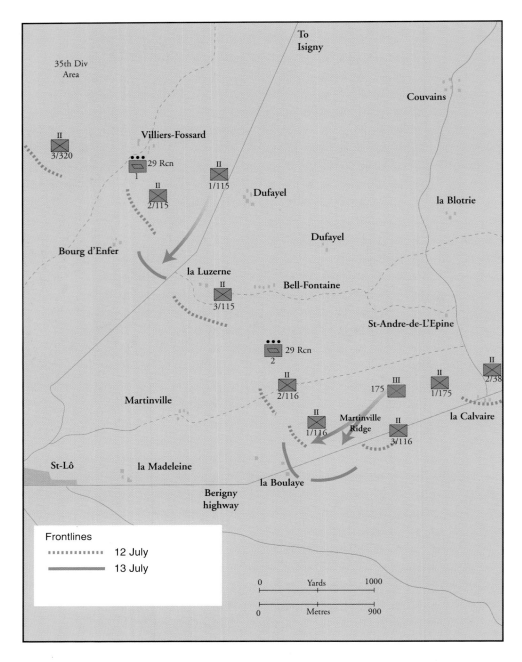

35th Div
Area

To
Isigny

Couvains

II
3/320

Villiers-Fossard

●●●
1 29 Rcn

II
2/115

II
1/115

Dufayel

la Blotrie

Bourg d'Enfer

Dufayel

la Luzerne

II
3/115

Bell-Fontaine

St-Andre-de-L'Epine

●●●
2 29 Rcn

Martinville

II
2/116

175

III
175

II
1/175

II
2/38

II
1/116

Martinville
Ridge

II
3/116

la Calvaire

St-Lô

la Madeleine

la Boulaye

Berigny
highway

Frontlines

┈┈┈┈┈┈┈ 12 July

━━━━━━━ 13 July

0   Yards   1000

0   Metres   900

the 11th, it attacked with a "rolling barrage" on the 12th, and managed to drive through the church and the surrounding houses. The 3rd Battalion bypassed the church and cemetery, though once again it ran into stubborn resistance farther south and made very little progress.

The 2nd Battalion continued to engage the Germans in a bitter house-to-house fight around the stone buildings of La Petite Ferme, which changed hands several times during the course of the afternoon. The two M-10 tank destroyers that had been attached to each battalion proved unable to destroy the stubbornly held enemy positions in the hedgerows. Progress for the regiment was once again measured in yards as the 320th Infantry advanced

■ *Above:* A rifle squad makes its way past vehicle wreckage on the country roads around St-Lô. The frontline was fluid around the town and enemy action continued despite reports that US troops had "cleared" positions.

■ *Left:* The 29th Division's attack from Martinville Ridge, 12–13 July.

about 274m (300 yards) from its second start position.

On 13 July, the two attacking regiments of the 35th Infantry Division renewed the offensive making only limited gains. Here, the Germans had employed an elaborate defence-in-depth scheme, whereby defensive outposts had been constructed and manned by small combat assault groups armed with mortars and machine guns. Both the 2nd Battalion, 137th Infantry, and the 1st Battalion, 320th Infantry, were to hit the centre of this elaborate German defensive network near le Carillon.

The same day, the 2nd Battalion of the 137th attacked south astride the stream flanking the positions on the west – G Company on the left and E on

the right. Each attacking battalion had at its disposal a platoon of heavy machine guns and a section of 81mm mortars attached (a platoon of medium tanks was available for the battalion). Tactics consisted of putting heavy concentrations of mortar fire on suspected enemy positions, followed by groups of four or five riflemen who attacked with an ample supply of hand and rifle grenades with the goal of working their way around enemy positions.

This seemed to be the solution as Company E progressed 548m (600 yards) by the end of the day, though Company G still met heavy opposition as it only moved 320m (350 yards) from its start position. German artillery, machine-gun and mortar fire still

■ *Above:* Around the village of St-Germain near Periers, 32km (20 miles) east of St-Lô, a squad of an armoured cavalry unit makes its way through flooded ground defended by *Fallschirmjaeger.*

■ *Opposite:* The 23rd Infantry Division at Hill 192, 11 July.

harried the attackers from the heights that dominated to the southeast. When the attack continued on 14 July, the rifle companies of both regiments measured their advances in the number of hedgerows they destroyed and not in yards, as German resistance intensified. When the battalion commander from the 2nd Battalion, 137th Infantry, attempted a wider envelopment the GIs met with stiff German resistance. As for the 320th Infantry, it made even less headway as resistance once again proved to be overwhelming as German forces, with the assistance of observers located on top of Hill 122, were able to call in artillery and mortars to pound the attacking Americans.

Meanwhile, on 14 July, even as it now appeared that the Americans had

finally cracked the Wehrmacht's MLR. XIX Corps ordered the 35th to make the main effort towards the Vire. In accordance with these plans, General Baade ordered the 137th Regiment to attack in line. With the 1st Battalion in the centre with the 3rd Battalion on its right, and each battalion supported by a platoon of Sherman tanks, a platoon of M-10 tank destroyers and division artillery, the attack commenced at 08:00 hours through a thick minefield and in a steady downpour. Almost as soon as the attack commenced, both battalions came under withering German artillery fire, primarily from 88mm guns, as well as blistering machine-gun fire. The M-10s, which operated as assault guns, placed heavy fire on the hedgerows just in front of the infantry, and managed to

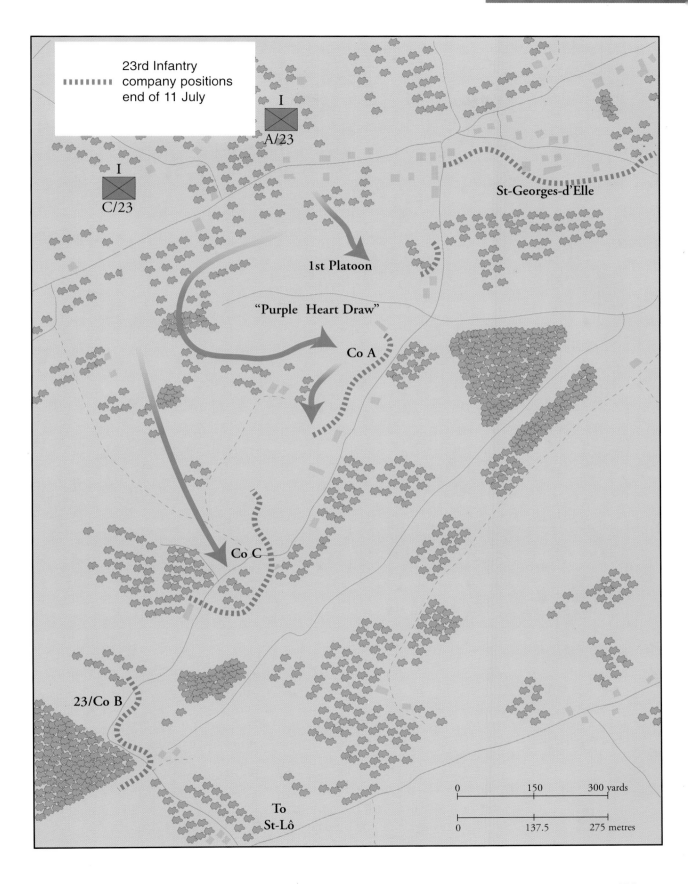

23rd Infantry company positions end of 11 July

I
A/23

I
C/23

St-Georges-d'Elle

1st Platoon

"Purple Heart Draw"

Co A

Co C

23/Co B

To St-Lô

| 0 | 150 | 300 yards |

| 0 | 137.5 | 275 metres |

■ *Above:* P-47
fighter-bomber
pilots pose around
the results of their
work: a shattered
Mk V Panther tank.

knock out about 19 machine gun emplacements and 4 mortar positions. The ferocity of the American attack finally broke the German line of resistance late in the day as the 1st and 3rd Battalions broke through to the Pont Hebert-St-Lô highway. Once again, however, the cost of success was high, as 125 soldiers were lost along with 11 Sherman tanks. The 35th had, however, managed to crack finally the German defences. This in turn caused a further rupture in Seventh Army's stand-fast orders from Field Marshal von Kluge. By undermining the German defences and cracking the German MLR, which had been manned primarily by the remnants of the depleted 352nd Division, who were dependent on its flanks holding for security, the 35th Division's breakthrough on 14 July assured XIX Corps that Hill 122 could not hold out much longer against the combined

American pressure now advancing across a broad front. General Baade now concentrated his forces against the 352nd for the final assault on Hill 122.

Meanwhile, having outflanked the German strongpoint at Carillon, the 137th Infantry now threatened Hill 122 with a pincer movement that would form a double envelopment of Carillon and Hill 122. In order to accomplish this, General Corlett released the 134th Infantry from corps reserve and directed Baade to take the heights. To succeed, Baade intended to attack with both flank regiments. While the 320th contained the Germans at le Carillon, the 137th was to advance across the Pont Hebert-St-Lô road. The 134th Infantry Regiment, commanded by Colonel Butler B. Miltonberger, was to move forward in direct assault against Hill 122. Success on the flanks would neutralize the Carillon position, eliminate Hill 122 and open the way for an easy advance to the final divisional objective: the stretch of the River Vire between the loop and the bend.

The Germans were not yet beaten, as they managed to inflict 117 casualties on the 137th Infantry as the 35th Division renewed the attack. It was now up to the 134th Infantry, which after meeting the same fierce enemy resistance, was able to fight its way into the cluster of farm buildings at Emelie behind a rolling barrage. By the afternoon the 134th had control of the entire hamlet at Emelie. By the evening, Brigadier-General Edmund B. Sebree, along with elements from the 737th Tank Battalion and a company of the 60th Engineer Battalion formed into a mobile task force, fought against stiff opposition to reach the top of Hill 122. After repelling a heavy German counterattack in the early hours of 16 July, Hill 122 was securely in the hands of the 35th Division.

The capture of Hill 122 by the 35th Division signalled the beginning of the end of the Battle for St-Lô and, more importantly, for the *bocage* country itself. For with the bastion of Hill 122 lost, the German defences around St-Lô began to crumble. By 17 July, the 137th Infantry had finally managed to break across the Pont Hebert-St-Lô ridge road in its drive south towards the River Vire. Meanwhile, the 320th Infantry mopped up the Carillon area, now almost abandoned by the Germans.[9]

Hobb's Division

As the 29th and 35th Divisions continued to press their attacks towards St-Lô, the 30th Division continued to press towards its objective – the north-south ridge between the Taute and Terrete Rivers. As the division moved towards the Terrete, the entrenched German defences intertwined with the hedgerows continued to be a source of consternation for General Hobbs as his forces battled their way along the open flanks of the river. Murderous enemy fire held back both his armour and infantry as they attempted to reach the Pont Hebert-Belle-Lande area and secure the bridge on the St-Lô highway. Here, elements of II Parachute Corps, 2nd SS Panzer Division, 902nd Panzergrenadier Regiment (of Panzer *Lehr*) and 3rd Parachute Division's Reconnaissance Battalion had been located. In fact, as the 30th Division's G-2 now believed, the division had stepped on a virtual "hornet's nest" as it reported the 30th was attacking into the "eye" of the storm in what appeared to be the reserve sector for the 2nd SS Panzer Division. By 14 July, after a three-day attack in which the division suffered heavy casualties, General Hobbs ordered the division to stand fast as preparations were being made for the final lunge towards St-Lô as part of the First Army's overall breakout plan.

For General Bradley, the taking of St-Lô was the key to his plan to break out of the Normandy countryside and begin the march towards the Seine. In a staff meeting with Field Marshal Montgomery on 27 June, Bradley and the commander of the Twenty-First Army Group agreed that the main thrust towards the Seine would be delivered by the US First Army while Lieutenant-General Miles C. Dempsey's British Second Army would continue to hold down the German panzer units in and around Caen.[10] Once again, the fighting would depend the tenacity of the American GI and his ability to overcome the stiffened German resistance.

The Capture of St-Lô

With the capture of Hill 122 by the soldiers of the 35th Division, the troops believed, as did their commanding officers, that the capture of St-Lô and an end to hedgerow fighting was close at hand. This proved to be an illusion, as the soldiers of the 115th Infantry discovered when they resumed the attack on 15 July along the Isigny-St-Lô road, and the 116th Infantry struck out along the crest of the Martinville Ridge. Shortly after the attack resumed, it once again got bogged down, due in part to enemy fire and as a result of poor command and control by higher headquarters. Despite the diversionary close air support attacks provided by IX Tactical Air Command and the 175th Infantry, the 116th Infantry lost seven medium tanks to enfilading enemy fire from the south. Lack of communications with the 35th Infantry Division caused the troops of the 115th Infantry to fire on American troops belonging to the 35th. Even as General Gerhardt exhorted his men forward and told them that, "come hell or high water", the division would keep moving towards St-Lô, the 29th Division's attack stalled in the face of increased German resistance.

■ *Right:* An M-5 Stuart motors past a line of German prisoners heading for the coast. Notice the white aircraft recognition symbol on the back of the tank.

Unknown to General Gerhardt, however, two assault battalions of the 116th had been making good progress along the Martinville Ridge when the 29th Division Headquarters, fearing its units might be cut off, ordered a halt for the night. While one battalion complied with the order, the other one, commanded by Major Sydney V. Bingham, Jr., had been unable to communicate with its advance units, which were in the process of organizing positions astride the Berigny highway less than 914m (1000 yards) from the edge of St-Lô.

A Steel Rain

German artillery and mortar fire opened up on Major Bingham's battalion shortly afterwards, and despite a series of fierce counterattacks launched by German infantry throughout that night, the American GIs tenaciously held onto their gains. In fact, so severe was the German fire from artillery, mortars and automatic weapons that attempts by both regiments to reach the isolated American battalion were blocked. So vulnerable was Bingham's unit thought to be that most American commanders felt that any attempt to rescue it would be suicidal. Yet both Americans and Germans alike saw the battalion's presence as an indication that the battle for St-Lô was nearly over.

Yet as Generals Corlett, Gerhardt and Hobbs conceded, German resistance was still too strong, as indicated by the failure of all three divisions to make substantial progress against the Martinville Ridge and the defences of St-Lô themselves. In short, there was some doubt as to whether or

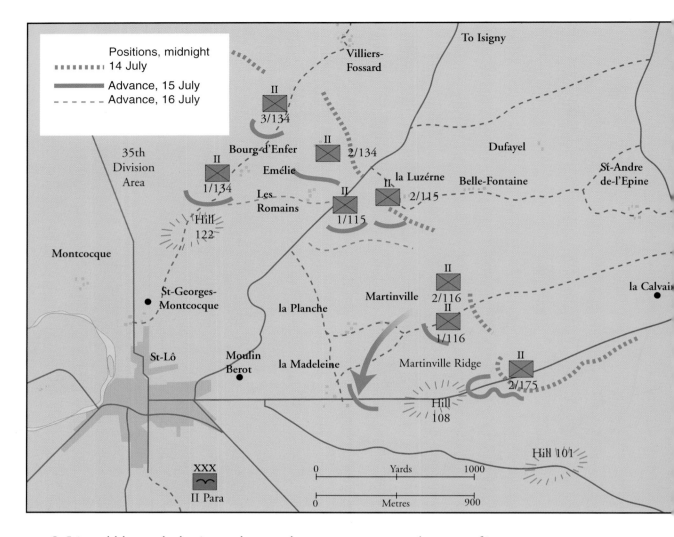

Positions, midnight
14 July

Advance, 15 July

Advance, 16 July

To Isigny

Villiers-Fossard

II 3/134

II 2/134

Bourg d'Enfer

Dufayel

35th Division Area

II 1/134

Emélie

Les Romains

II 1/115

II la Luzérne

Belle-Fontaine

St-Andre de-l'Epine

2/115

Hill 122

Montcocque

St-Georges-Montcocque

la Planche

Martinville

II 2/116

II 1/116

la Calvai

St-Lô

Moulin Berot

la Madeleine

Martinville Ridge

II 2/175

Hill 108

Hill 101

XXX
II Para

0   Yards   1000

0   Metres   900

not St-Lô could be reached prior to the commencement of Operation Cobra – General Bradley's bold plan to break out of the Normandy countryside. General Bradley needed St-Lô primarily in order to control the River Vire crossing site there to block German counterattacks against the flank of his push out of Normandy. Thus, it was vital to bring the battle of St-Lô to an end, even it meant continuing the advance at a snail's pace and eliminating every enemy occupied hedgerow in the process.

While the 29th Division came the closest to taking St-Lô, continued fighting had weakened the unit considerably. The 116th Infantry had received an infusion of 125 combat replacements to restore at least one of its assault battalions, but it was still only at 60 percent of its authorized combat strength. Despite the fact that on the night of 16/17 July the 116th received 250 more replacements, its strength of 420 officers and men remained far below the authorized strength of an American combat regiment. The 115th Infantry's strength was not much better, since one of its rifle battalions had only a platoon of riflemen remaining in each rifle company. On 17 July, the day before the final offensive into St-Lô began, some 200 men made up the three rifle companies of the 175th Infantry, with most of its commissioned and noncommissioned officers having

■ *Above:* Having secured the ridge and road east of St-Lô, the 29th Division, supported by the 35th, began an advance from the north. Its next major objective was Hill 122. The 35th Division's 134th Infantry would lead the assault on 16 July.

either been killed or wounded. While these three regiments remained extreme cases, other infantry battalions faced similar shortages of trained riflemen.[11]

In order to take St-Lô, General Gerhardt turned to the use of mechanized forces and armour. He therefore instructed Brigadier-General Norman Cota to form a task force comprised of tanks, tank destroyers, reconnaissance or light tanks, armoured cars and engineer troops. This force was to assemble in the division's rear, positioned towards a location that would facilitate its advance towards the Isigny-St-Lô highway, or east down the Martinville Ridge.[12]

On 17 July, the 29th Division renewed the attack towards St-Lô, and undertake the relief of Major Bingham's isolated battalion. To reach Bingham's command, General Gerhardt ordered Major Thomas D. Howie's 3rd Battalion, 116th Infantry, to attempt the rescue. After crawling through a hailstorm of German artillery and mortar fire, Major Howie's force finally reached Bingham's unit. Colonel Philip R. Dwyer, the commanding officer of the 116th Infantry, then ordered both units to begin the advance into St-Lô. Major Howie informed Colonel Dwyer that Bingham's force was in no condition to continue offensive operations for the time being. The major responded enthusiastically in the affirmative, however, when asked by Dwyer if his men could make the first

■ *Below:* At a forward medical station barely a mile from the front, line corpsmen give emergency aid before the wounded are sent back to the hospital ships for their trip back to England.

push into the town. Several minutes later, however, a German shell killed Major Howie. His executive officer, Captain William H. Puntenny, then assumed command of the battalion, and shortly thereafter reorganized the battalion and mounted the attack on St-Lô along the Berigny highway.

After moving several hundred yards towards the town's edge, German artillery and mortar fire plastered the advancing American troops and threatened to cut them off from the rest of the 29th Division. Also in trouble was one battalion of the 115th Infantry, acting as the regiment's central force, which had managed to advance to the northeast outskirts of St-Lô on the afternoon of the 17th and had run into blistering German fire. Exasperated and under pressure from General Corlett to effect a breakthrough, XIX Corps'

■ *Above:* The hedgerows could also lend some useful cover from sudden German bombardment. From the look of their gear these men have not been in the line very long.

commander told the 115th's regimental commander that the division's advance depended on this one battalion entering the town, and that if necessary he was to expend the whole battalion to achieve this crucial mission. By nightfall of 17 July, the troops of the 115th Infantry were near the northeastern fringe of the town, but in getting there they had taken horrendous losses and was near exhaustion.

Convinced that the only feasible point of entry to St-Lô was the northeastern gate, General Gerhardt changed his week-long scheme of manoeuvre. For the final drive into St-Lô the commanding general of the 29th Division ordered the two regiments on the left – those on Martinville Ridge – to hold their positions while the 115th Infantry made the final lunge. After some consternation, due largely to the division's repeated assaults throughout hedgerow country and more importantly around the heights surrounding St-Lô, General Corlett ordered General Gerhardt to take the town without further delay.

The German Position

For the Germans, the situation at St-Lô was becoming more hopeless by the hour. Added to this, as on the opposing side with the American high command, there was tension between various German headquarters. Colonel-General Hausser, realizing that the St-Lô sector was now indefensible, requested permission from OB West (Von Kluge) and OKW (Jodl) to withdraw in order to form a new defensive line just outside the town to the south. Surprisingly, an operations officer at OKW in Berlin informed Hausser, in direct contradiction to Adolf Hitler's standing order to hold fast, that he was to take whatever measures he thought necessary to withdraw. After he had done so he was told to report that the enemy had penetrated his main line of resistance in several places, and that he had been able to re-establish a new line only with the greatest difficulty!

Added to the severe attrition of German troops defending St-Lô and its surrounding heights, the inability of Panzer *Lehr* to prevent the 30th Division from advancing towards its objective, as well as the failure of II Parachute Corps to re-establish its defensive lines north of St-Lô, made it impossible to prevent a possible encirclement of Wehrmacht forces inside the town. With the operational and tactical situation deteriorating at an increasing rate, the Germans also lost the services of their best field commander, Field Marshal Erwin Rommel, who had been severely wounded in a strafing attack by an Allied plane on 17 July.

■ *Right:* A motorized column comes to a sudden halt as German artillery fire from around St-Lô claims a direct hit on a command truck.

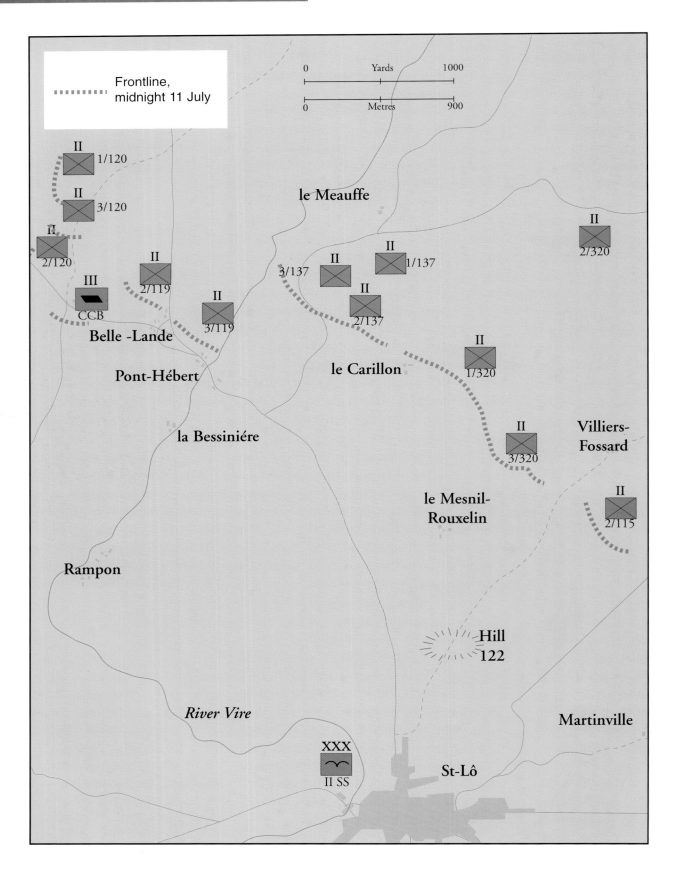

Frontline,
midnight 11 July

0   Yards   1000

0   Metres   900

II
1/120

II
3/120

II
2/120

III
CCB

le Meauffe

II
2/119

II
3/119

II
3/137

II
1/137

II
2/137

II
1/320

II
2/320

le Carillon

Belle -Lande

Pont-Hébert

la Bessiniére

Rampon

II
3/320

Villiers-
Fossard

le Mesnil-
Rouxelin

II
2/115

Hill
122

River Vire

XXX
II SS

St-Lô

Martinville

■ *Above:* After
weeks of fighting
to gain control of
this vital position,
St-Lô itself was left
an utter ruin. The
First Army's
breakout into
France would not
have been possible
without control of
this communica-
tions centre.

■ *Left:* The
siuation north of
St-Lô on 11 July
1944.

Succeeded by Field Marshal von
Kluge, who assumed direct tactical
command of Army Group B as well as
retaining command of OB West, the
veteran panzer commander sought to
prevent a complete rupture of the
German position in Normandy.

After OKW had informed General
Jodl of Hausser's withdrawal, Kluge
attempted with little success to avert a
complete breakdown of the Seventh
Army's main line of resistance at St-Lô.
The field marshal ordered Hausser to
keep the Americans out of the town,
though he had very few reserves left to
send him to carry out this order. The
5th Parachute Division, which had only
a few days before arrived from Brittany,
was already committed to the fight in
support of Panzer *Lehr*. The 275th
Division likewise had not reached the

St-Lô area to become a factor, while
Panzer Group West continued to
reinforce positions in and around Caen.
In fact, in order to bolster the defences
around St-Lô, General of Infantry Hans
Speidel suggested to Field Marshal von
Kluge that the 1st SS Panzer Division
Leibstandarte be transferred to that sector.
Von Kluge refused this request, insisting
that the 1st SS Panzer Division was to
remain in and around Caen since, "he
was already planning a major spoiling
attack against the British forces in the
Caen sector in which both 1st and 2nd
SS Panzer Divisions were to be used."[13]

As Colonel-General Hausser
marshalled what forces he could to
prevent a complete rupture of the
German positions, the US 29th Infantry
Division readied itself for the final drive
into St-Lô. After informing General

Cota to be ready to move, General Gerhardt issued the order to advance into the town early in the afternoon of 18 July. After departing from its assembly area, the armoured task force from the 29th Infantry Division proceeded down the Isigny-St-Lô highway. After meeting scattered opposition in the form of antitank and rifle fire, the 1st Battalion, 115th Infantry, entered the northeastern section of the town. Meanwhile, elements of the 35th Division finally made the final successful lunge towards Hill 122, which it secured at the same time as General Cota's Task Force C entered St-Lô.

Parthian Shots

German opposition was not yet finished, however, as Hausser ordered an immediate counterattack to retake the town. German artillery and mortar fire smashed into the American lines as the 352nd Division launched a counterattack against the advancing American forces. Too weak to expel the Americans, and unable to secure further reinforcements, Hausser's forces broke off the attack leaving the 29th and 35th Divisions in full control of St-Lô. The German 352nd Division, beaten though not defeated, continued to "jab" at the Americans inside St-Lô as it launched several more counterattacks that evening and over the next few days. It was a reminder to General Corlett and his subordinate commanders that they had not gone very far. On 20 July, the soldiers of the 29th nonetheless continued the final phase of the campaign by mopping up small groups of German soldiers that had stayed on to fight. Even as General Gerhardt contacted General Cota by telephone that St-Lô was in American hands, XIX Corps' commander informed his subordinate that it was too late: "NBC radio beat you to it!"

The eight-day campaign to take St-Lô was not without its cost. In the fighting the 29th Division had suffered over 3000 casualties, while the 35th had incurred 2000 casualties. A stark reminder of the sacrifice of the fighting for St-Lô was the death of Major Howie, whose body had been transported into the town on orders from General Gerhardt and placed inside a Catholic Church in the town draped in an American flag, in order to remind the troops of the sacrifices by thousands of their comrades-in-arms who had died in hedgerow country since 6 June.

Summary

After eight days of fighting the soldiers of the US First Army had achieved their first major objective in General Bradley's overall scheme of breakout from the Normandy beaches. The casualty figures point out that this was no easy feat of arms. Indeed, the fighting in and around the Carentan-Cotentin Peninsula demonstrated that the German Army was far from defeated, and that it had not, in fact, disintegrated in the face of the overwhelming Allied assault on 6 June. While it was beaten, General Hausser's Seventh Army had not been defeated and was still capable of offensive operations.

Tactically, the fight for St-Lô, and for all of the hedgerow country, demonstrated the necessity for combined arms in the attack. While General Bradley's adoption of a "broad front" strategy at first seemed to hold the key to overwhelming the German defenders in the *bocage* country and the successful push into St-Lô during the early days of the Normandy landings, it was instead Field Marshal Montgomery's field-tested methodology of attacking along a narrow front with combined-arms teams that won the battle of the hedgerows. Only when XIX Corps

adopted the principles of dealing with each individual hedgerow as a set-piece battle, rather than expose American troops piecemeal to murderous small-arms fire, were casualties reduced. As General Bradley sought to capitalize on the strategic objectives of Overlord, Field Marshal Montgomery realized that the war in Northwest Europe would not be won with "giant sweeps" but through a series of carefully planned operations fought in set-piece battles, as occurred in the *bocage* country of Normandy in June and July of 1944.[14]

This is not a flaw of generalship on General Bradley's part. Schooled in the methods of attrition warfare, he had more resources to throw at the German defenders in the hedgerows. General Bradley fought the campaign in the *bocage* country with vigour and resourcefulness, and utilized the men

■ *Above:* With the fighting in the *bocage* behind them, in early August US armour start the great drive south and east through what is left of St-Lô. The ruined panzer is a Mk IV.

195

and materiel at his disposal to the best of his professional abilities. As General Eisenhower later conceded in a letter to General George C. Marshall, Chairman of the US Joint Chiefs of Staff, several features contributed to the fight in Normandy during July 1944. These factors, Eisenhower outlined to General Marshall, included: "First, as always, the fighting quality of the German soldier;

second the nature of the terrain; third, the weather." [15]

In sum, a combination of factors contributed to the fighting in the *bocage*. As the Americans discovered, the pre-D-Day intelligence summaries had, in fact, made mention of the *bocage* country. However, no one made any great effort to prepare US ground forces for the possibility of fighting a well-

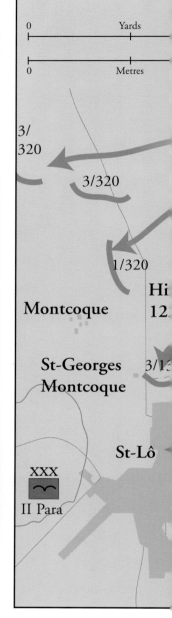

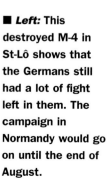

■ *Left:* This destroyed M-4 in St-Lô shows that the Germans still had a lot of fight left in them. The campaign in Normandy would go on until the end of August.

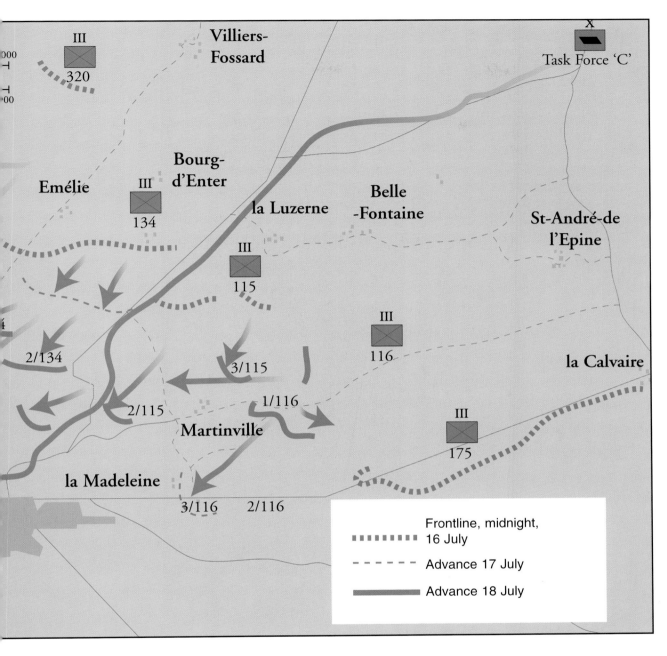

Villiers-Fossard

III
320

Emélie

Bourg-d'Enter

III
134

la Luzerne

Belle-Fontaine

St-André-de l'Epine

III
115

2/134

III
116

la Calvaire

3/115

1/116

2/115

Martinville

III
175

la Madeleine

3/116   2/116

Task Force 'C'

	Frontline, midnight, 16 July
	Advance 17 July
	Advance 18 July

entrenched German Army there. Second, over-confidence allowed American commanders to assume that the German Army, which had been capable of mounting only local counter-attacks immediately after D-Day, was for all intents and purposes defeated. This had tragic consequences as American GIs soon discovered as they walked into an elaborate defence-in-depth network constructed with the help of nature and French farms. The Germans were able to organize their excellent firepower into a strong defence-in-depth network in order to delay, and in some instances halt, the advancing Americans. German defences in the hedgerows proved that the Wehrmacht was the master of defence and that the war in Northwest Europe

■ *Above:* The infantry regiments of XXX Corps, having cleared the hills and ridges around the town, had to leave the capture of St-Lô to Task Force 'C'.

was far from over. Also, while histories of the campaign have often slighted the German defenders as being second-echelon troops, the fact remained that apart from the *Osttruppen*, the regular Wehrmacht units proved that they still possessed "staying power" and were far from beaten. As for the élite Waffen-SS armoured and panzergrenadier units, they demonstrated to the end that they would, indeed, fight to the death in defence of the Reich and would give no quarter nor ask for any.

The Weather

Lastly, as General Eisenhower conceded, the weather during this phase of the Normandy campaign proved to be extremely uncooperative, as rain, mud and fog hampered Allied air operations and resupply efforts. The rain and mud of the *bocage* country made fighting all the more difficult as the soaked and tired GIs trudged from one hedgerow to another, only to go through the same routine of blasting and scraping the enemy from his earthen defences, in what seemed to be an endless series of small-unit firefights against an enemy determined to defend them to the death. As one American GI concluded after the battle: "We won the battle of Normandy . . . [but] . . . considering the high price in American lives, we lost." [16]

Despite the appalling losses in the fight for the "bloody *bocage*", General Bradley set out to implement phase two of his breakout campaign designed to send American armour to the River Seine and beyond. At last he could put behind him one of the bloodiest periods in American military history.

■ *Right:* After the German line around St-Lô broke, in early August VII Corps turned east and south towards Coutances in a huge flanking move that would end at Falaise south of Caen.

CHAPTER VI:

CONCLUSION

The tactical lessons of the *bocage* campaign. The reasons for the German defeat. The final cost to both sides.

The fight in Normandy's *bocage* country illustrated the problems American commanders had experienced since the US Army first entered combat in North Africa in 1943. While General Bradley and others had counted upon the overwhelming superiority and numerical advantage of American arms, fighting the Germans in the hedgerows demonstrated that war was still the domain of the infantryman and his supporting arms.

The elaborate German defences in the hedgerows presented American infantry and combined-arms commanders with problems that often negated the "school solution" of overwhelming the enemy with fire and manoeuvre, with little consideration given to the need for a unified combined-arms doctrine.

Indeed, as the German defenders in the hedgerows reminded the attacking American soldiers time and again, it was the defender and not attacker that decided when, where and how the battle would proceed. By selecting the hedgerow country of Normandy to make its first stand against the US First Army, the Wehrmacht briefly immobilized the overwhelming American advantage in tanks, vehicles and other mechanized assets and forced the US Army to fight on its terms and over terrain of its choosing.

The result was that the Americans had to fight for nearly every hedgerow, that the Germans had transformed into a

■ *Left:* The beginning of Operation Cobra, 25 July 1944: the moment when the Normandy campaign changed from an infantrymen's fight to a great armoured charge across an 8km (4.5-mile) front into the heart of France.

mini-fortress. The hedges had to be dealt with by set-piece assault teams in a laborious and time-consuming process that delayed General Bradley's desire to avoid the attrition-style of warfare of World War I. The savagery of the fighting in the *bocage* can be seen in the American casualties incurred in three weeks of fighting. According to Field Marshal Montgomery, the American casualty figures were quite staggering, and reflected the nature of the fighting in the "bloody *bocage*" of Normandy:

American Weekly Losses in the *Bocage*

To	Wounded	Killed
22 June 1944	15,362	3012
10 July 1944	32,443	6898
19 July 1944	51,387	10,641

The above figures show that Field Marshal Montgomery's later statement that the battle of Normandy, "was fought exactly as planned before the

■ *Below:* To the east of the US First Army, the British VIII and XXX Corps south of Bayeux began their own push south in Operation Bluecoat.

■ *Right:* With the roads out of St-Lô now free of Germans, the armoured columns of VII Corps began heading for the next major road junction, at the town of Coutances.

invasion" is incorrect. No planner prior to the landings could have foreseen the difficulties faced by American troops in the *bocage* country, and if they did then the troops were needlessly thrown into the battle unprepared for the ordeal of combat ahead. General Bradley was more correct in his summation that the only alternative for the Allies (British and American forces) was to "smash through" the German frontline defences, since only a "breakout" would effect a rupture of the enemy lines to enable the American and British forces to utilize their advantages in mobility in a war of manoeuvre.

While the debate between Montgomery and Bradley continued on in the battle of the postwar memoirs as to whose methods were instrumental in the defeat of the German Army during the battle for Normandy, the fact remained that the fighting in the *bocage* country once again brought to the fore the importance of combined arms and the requirements of modern mechanized warfare. This was a fact that had become apparent once in the *bocage*, as it showed that American commanders had neglected to prepare adequately their forces for combat in Northwest Europe. While the prewar US Army field regulations made specific mention of the need to train troops in combined-arms warfare, the fact remained that the lessons of the débâcle at Kasserine Pass in February 1943 had not been completely absorbed by American field commanders, specifically General Bradley himself, as the GIs prepared for Overlord. In fact, General Bradley made little mention or reference to the lessons of Kasserine Pass as applied to preparing the US Army for its grim

ordeal in Northwest Europe. Indeed, what occurred in the *bocage* country only reinforced the fact that combined-arms training had been seriously neglected in preparing the US Army for combat in France. This proved to be decisive for both the way the campaign was fought in the hedgerows and throughout the remainder of the campaign in France and into Germany.

The need for more effective tank-infantry teams was among the most vital lessons learned in the *bocage* fighting, particularly as US forces began to approach the Siegfried Line. While US commanders became absorbed in the planning and execution of the breakout from Normandy and the rapid movement across France, there was agreement in the after-action reports that the experience gained in Normandy demonstrated the need for closer cooperation between the different combat arms.

In a tactical sense, the First Army proved initially ineffective in its first major battle with the main elements of the Wehrmacht during the fighting in the hedgerows. The elaborate German defences in the Normandy farmland, demonstrated that it was the rifleman with supporting arms backed up by an excellent logistical and support system behind him that won battles, and not grand strategy. In the *bocage* fighting, the common denominator between the Americans and Germans was the emphasis the fighting placed on individual combat skills, with advances measured hedgerow by hedgerow and not by large sweeps made or arrows drawn on a map board in a command post or combat operations centre.

■ *Left:* As enemy defences buckled, units of the 4th Armored Division reached Coutances on 30 July, only to find that the Germans had already left.

■ *Right:* General Patton took command of VIII Corps and on 30 July launched a drive south, taking Avranches – and these prisoners – on the same day.

As for the Germans, only their adoption of elaborate defensive tactics in the hedgerows had averted what they later admitted could have been a total disintegration of their defences in Normandy. Only by constantly shifting its forces over terrain that channelled the US First Army's broad-front strategy did the Wehrmacht avoid total defeat. Nonetheless, the fact remained that the inability to bring sufficient forces to bear greatly hindered the Germans from capitalizing on their success by concentrating their forces against the various American armies in the *bocage*. Had the Germans been able to concentrate any one portion their forces against any one of the American divisions in the area outside of St-Lô they just might have turned the course of battle in any one sector. However, they were forced to contain local thrusts in order to relieve pressure on their own frontline units.

One other factor contributed to the German defeat in the battle of the *bocage*, and that was the lack of aggressiveness displayed by some units in making wholehearted offensive efforts. There was solid evidence for this, at least in the views held by Rommel and the other senior German officers concerning the results of Panzer *Lehr*'s attack of 11 July 1944. This was noted in the US Army's official history, which stated that there was some dissatisfaction at the high command echelons with overall panzer effectiveness. Fighting spirit was the vital prerequisite for success, and there were signs that it was eroding at troop level.

Part of the "lack of spirit" can be attributed to the shortages the Germans

experienced in both men and materiel. Although German troop morale was good, courage alone could not compensate for materiel disadvantage. In short, the Germans could not meet the Allied rate of fire because their transportation system had been bombed incessantly by Allied aircraft night and day, as well as being the target for raids by the French resistance.

Costly in men and materiel as hedgerow fighting was for the Allies, it was equally expensive for the Germans, who simply could not replace or replenish their forces in a way the First Army could. In an official report issued from OB West in the autumn of 1944, the German high command reported that it had lost 150 Mk IV tanks, 85 Mk V Panthers, 15 Tiger Is, 167 75mm assault guns (Mk IIIs and Mk IVs), and almost 30 88mm dual-purpose guns between 6 June and 9 July – more than enough to equip an entire Waffen-SS division.

The price in manpower for the Germans was even more staggering. Between 6 June and 11 July, at the start of General Bradley's drive towards St-

■ *Above:* Breaking through Avranches, the next objective was Ducey to the south, from where led the roads towards the Third Army's first objective, the Atlantic ports of Brittany.

208

Lô, OB West lost some 2000 officers and 85,000 enlisted men. In the St-Lô-Cotentin sector, the 243rd Division alone lost over 8000 men, while the 352nd lost 8000 officers and men. Panzer *Lehr* lost some 3140 officers and enlisted men. By 17 July, total German casualties had risen to about 100,000, of which 2360 were officers. Despite Field Marshal von Kluge's desperate attempts at reinforcing the depleted units in Normandy, he sometimes wondered whether or not OKW appreciated the tremendous consumption of forces on big battle days his divisions were forced to confront during the fighting in the hedgerows.

While the battle in the hedgerows was an infantryman's war, von Kluge and other German commanders, including the former commanding officer of OB West, Field Marshal von Rundstedt, correctly saw Germany's only chance of repelling the US First Army was with an active mobile defence. Field Marshal von Kluge wanted "more tanks" to act as the "spine" for the German infantry to deal with any further Allied breakthrough. Unfortunately, Germany was now scraping the bottom of the barrel in order to stave off defeat in the East and the West. As the fighting in the *bocage* country ended, Field Marshal Montgomery's Twenty-First Army Group and General Bradley's First Army laid the foundation for the Allied victory in Northwest Europe, as they forced the Germans to concede that the Wehrmacht could never hope to match the Allies in terms of men and equipment, despite its superior tactical and operational abilities. Field Marshal Montgomery in his memoirs provided a rough estimate of the German losses during the battle for Normandy:

Right: In the first week of August in the XIX Corps area south of St-Lô, the 30th Infantry Division had taken the town of Domfront. As can be seen, Allied bombers and artillery had done their usual work.

German Losses: Battle of Normandy[1]
Corps and Divisional Commanders
Killed or Captured: 20

Army Commanders Wounded: 2
(Rommel, Hausser)

Supreme Commanders Dismissed: 2
(Von Rundstedt; Von Kluge)

Divisions Eliminated or Mauled: 40
Total Losses (Estimate): 300,000
Guns Captured or Destroyed: 3000
Tanks Destroyed: 1000

The Germans, nevertheless, did their best to contain the American breakthrough in Normandy. General Dwight D. Eisenhower acknowledged in his final report of the operations on the Cotentin Peninsula that for six weeks there followed, "a gruelling struggle to secure a lodgement area of sufficient depth in which to build up a striking force of such magnitude as to enable us to make full use of our potential material superiority. The process took longer than we expected, largely owing to the adverse weather conditions which repeatedly interrupted the flow of men and stores across the Channel. The enemy fought tenaciously to contain our beachheads, though he was at no time able to collect the strength to constitute a serious offensive threat."[2] Tactically and operationally, General Eisenhower admitted that due to the Wehrmacht's shortage in infantry, its leaders came to depend upon the use of tanks in a defensive role to strengthen its defences. This in turn prevented the Germans from using their qualitative advantage in tanks in more mobile operations, something that Field Marshal von Rundstedt had advocated long before the Allied landings in Normandy. It also prevented the Germans from pulling their armour

back to be used once an Allied breakthrough occurred. In one sense, General Eisenhower's comments gave credence to Field Marshal von Rundstedt's earlier conclusions prior to D-Day that a more mobile defence was the best way to defeat the landing, as opposed to Rommel's desire to fight from fixed positions around the beachhead.

As for the fighting in the *bocage* country itself, the view of Lieutenant-General Dietrich von Choltitz perhaps best summarized the fighting for both the American and German soldiers, when he commented that the fighting in Normandy in the summer of 1944 was, "a monstrous blood-bath", the like of which he had not seen in 11 years of war".[3] For the ordinary American GI, however, who through sheer endurance overcame the elaborate German defences in the hedgerows of Normandy, combat in the *bocage* country brought with it a renewed respect for his German adversary – a respect that remained with him throughout the remainder of the war.

■ *Below:* First Army M-10s pass through Fontainebleau on the open road to Paris, 23 August.

CHAPTER NOTES

CHAPTER I

1 Gordon A. Harrison, *United States Army in World War II: The European Theater of Operations: Cross-Channel Attack*, Reprinted. (Washington, D.C., Center of Military History, 1951 and 1989), p57. Hereafter cited as Harrison, *Cross-Channel Attack*.

2 Ibid, pp57–8.

3 General Omar N. Bradley, *A Soldier's Story*. Third Edition. (New York: Random House, 1999), pp317–8. Hereafter cited as Bradley, *A Soldier's Story*.

4 Ibid.

5 Michael D. Doubler, *Busting the Bocage: American Combined Arms Operations in France. 6 June–31 July 1944*, (Masters Thesis, The Ohio State University, Columbus, Ohio, 1985), p39. Hereafter cited as Doubler, *Busting the Bocage*.

6 Ibid, pp39–40.

7 General der Infanterie (Lieutenant General) Dr. Hans Speidel. *Invasion 1944: Rommel and the Normandy Campaign*. (Chicago: Henry Regnery Company, 1950), p. 35. Hereafter cited as Speidel, *Invasion 1944*.

8 Harrison, *Cross-Channel Attack*, p 237.

9 Ibid, p239.

10 Ibid, p240.

11 Equivalent to an American Army lieutenant-general. See Harrison, *Cross-Channel Attack*, Appendix H.

12 Speidel, *Invasion 1944*, p36.

13 Harrison, *Cross-Channel Attack*, p242.

14 Ibid, p248.

15 See Field Marshal Erwin Rommel, *The Rommel Papers*, Edited by B. H. Liddell Hart. (Norwalk, CT, The Easton Press, 1988), pp469–72. Hereafter cited as Rommel, *The Rommel Papers*.

16 Ibid, p469.

17 Harrison, *Cross-Channel Attack*, p258.

CHAPTER II

1 Doubler, *Busting the Bocage*, p54.

2 Ibid, p54.

3 Ibid, p54.

4 Ibid, p10.

5 Ibid, pp14–5.

6 See William O. Odom's, *After the Trenches: The Transformation of U.S. Army Doctrine, 1918–1939*. (College Station: Texas A & M Press, 1999) and; U.S. War Department, *Field Service Regulations: Operations, FM-100-5*. Reprinted by U.S. Army Command and General Staff College. (Fort Leavenworth: U.S. Army Command and General Staff College Press, 1992).

7 Ibid, p60.

8 See Stephen Hart's, *Montgomery and "Colossal Cracks," The 21st Army Group in Northwest Europe, 1944–1945*. (Westport, CT: Praeger Publishing Co., 2000) also; Field Marshal Sir Bernard L. Montgomery's *Normandy to the Baltic*. (Boston: Houghton Mifflin Co., 1948).

CHAPTER III

1 Harrison, *Cross-Channel Attack*, p375.

2 Ibid, p381.

3 Ibid, pp381–2.

4 Ibid, pp383–4.

5 Michael D. Doubler, *Closing With the Enemy. How GIs Fought the War in Europe, 1944–1945*. (Lawrence: University of Kansas Press, 1994), p49. Hereafter cited as Doubler, *Closing With the Enemy*.

6 Ibid, p46.

7 General Dwight D. Eisenhower, *Crusade in Europe*. (New York: Doubelday & Company, 1948), p.269. Hereafter cited as Eisenhower, *Crusade in Europe*.

8 Doubler, *Closing With the Enemy*, pp47–8.

9 Martin Blumenson, *United States Army in World War II: The European Theater of Operations: Breakout and Pursuit*. (Washington, D.C., Center for Military History, 1993), p43. Hereafter cited as Blumenson, *Breakout and Pursuit*.

10 Ibid, pp43–4.

11 Leon C. Standifer, *Not In Vain. A*

Rifleman Remembers World War II. (Baton Rouge: Louisiana State University Press: 1992), pp142–43.

CHAPTER IV

1 Rundstedt was replaced by Kluge by Hitler in the beginning of July. See Blumenson, *Breakout and Pursuit*, p47.
2 Bradley, *A Soldier's Story*, pp316–7.
3 Ibid, p318.
4 Montgomery, *Normandy to the Baltic*, p107.
5 Blumenson, *Breakout and Pursuit*, p65.
6 Ibid, p76.
7 U.S. War Department, *St.-Lô (7 July–19 July 1944)*. American Forces in Action Series. (Washington, D.C., Historical Division, War Department, 1946; Reprinted Washington, D.C., Center for Military History, 1994), p6. Hereafter cited as War Department, *St-Lô*.
8 Ibid, p7.
9 Ibid, pp16–7.
10 Blumenson, *Breakout and Pursuit*, p113.
11 War Department, *St-Lo*, p41.
12 Omar N. Bradley, and Clay Blair, *A General's Life. An Autobiography by General of the Army Omar N. Bradley and Clay Blair*. Second Edition. (Norwalk, CT: The Easton Press, 1995), p272. Hereafter cited as Bradley and Blair, *A General's Life*.

CHAPTER V

1 War Department, *St-Lô*, pp51–3.
2 Ibid, pp59–61.
3 Blumenson, *Breakout and Pursuit*, p150.
4 Ibid, p152.
5 Ibid, p154
6 War Department, *St-Lô*, p55.
7 Blumenson, *Breakout and Pursuit*, p157.
8 War Department, *St-Lô*, pp72–75.
9 Ibid, pp84–86; Blumenson, *Breakout and Pursuit*, pp160–3.
10 Bradley, *A Soldier's Story*, p319.
11 Blumenson, *Breakout and Pursuit*, p166.
12 Ibid.
13 See James J. Weingartner, *Hitler's Guard: The Story of the Leibstandarte SS Adolf Hitler 1933–1945.* (Carbondale: Southern Illinois University Press, 1968), pp104–5
14 See Hart, *Montgomery and Colossal Cracks*, pp85–8.
15 Blumenson, *Breakout and Pursuit*, p177.
16 Ibid, p176.

CHAPTER VI

1 Field Marshal, Sir B. L. Montgomery, *The Memoirs of Field Marshal The Viscount Montgomery of Alamen, K.G.* (Cleveland, OH/New York World Publishing Co., 1958), p231.
2 Montgomery, *Normandy to the Baltic*, p180, Bradley, *A Soldier's Story*, p318.
3 Blumenson, *Breakout and Pursuit*, p181.
4 Ibid, p.181; Robert L. Hewitt, *Work Horse of the Western Front: The Story of the 30th Infantry Division*. (Washington, D.C., Infantry Journal Press, 1946), p34.
5 Blumenson, *Breakout and Pursuit*, p181.
6 Montgomery, *Memoirs*, p236.
7 General Dwight D. Eisenhower, *Report by The Supreme Commander to the Combined Chiefs of Staff on the Operations in Europe of the Allied Expeditionary Force 6 June 1944 to 8 May 1945.* (Washington, D.C., Army Times, 1945), p28.
8 Ibid, p182.

CONCLUSION

1 Montgomery, *Normandy to the Baltic*, p236.
2 General Dwight D. Eisenhower, *Report by The Supreme Commander to the Combined Chiefs of Staff on the Operations in Europe of the Allied Expeditionary Force 6 June 1944 to 8 May 1945.* (Washington, D.C., Army Times, 1945), p28.
3 Blumenson, *Breakout and Pursuit*, p231.

US INFANTRY DIVISION (1943)

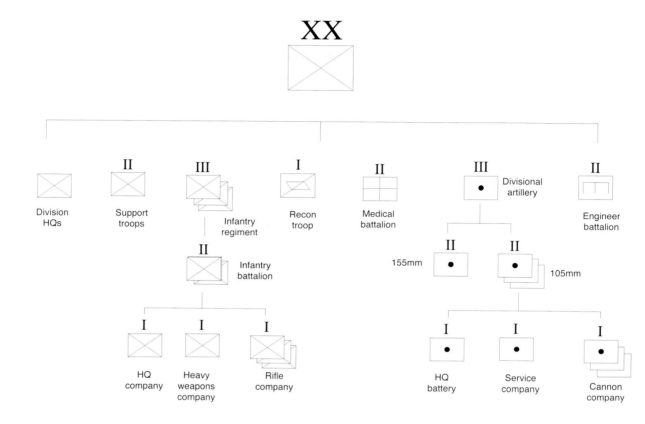

Officers: 761
Warrant officers: 44
Enlisted men: 13,238
TOTAL: 14,043

WEHRMACHT INFANTRY BATTALION (1944)

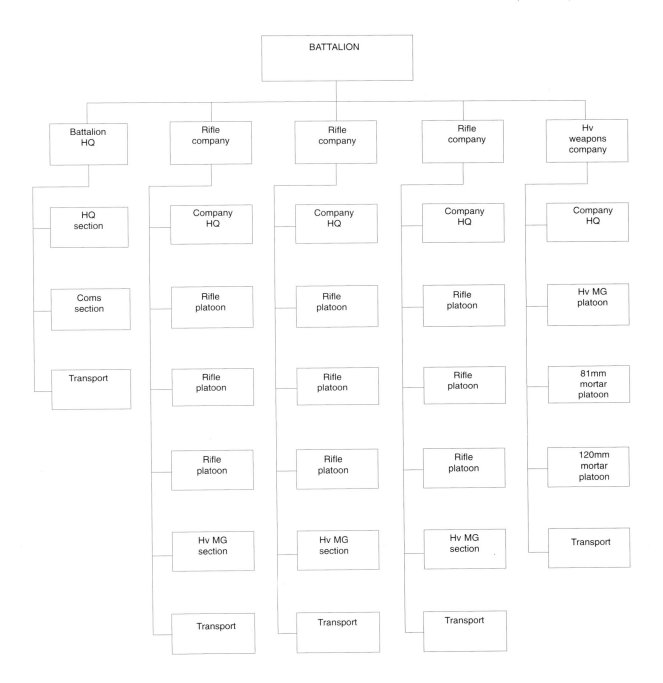

WEHRMACHT INFANTRY REGIMENT (1944)

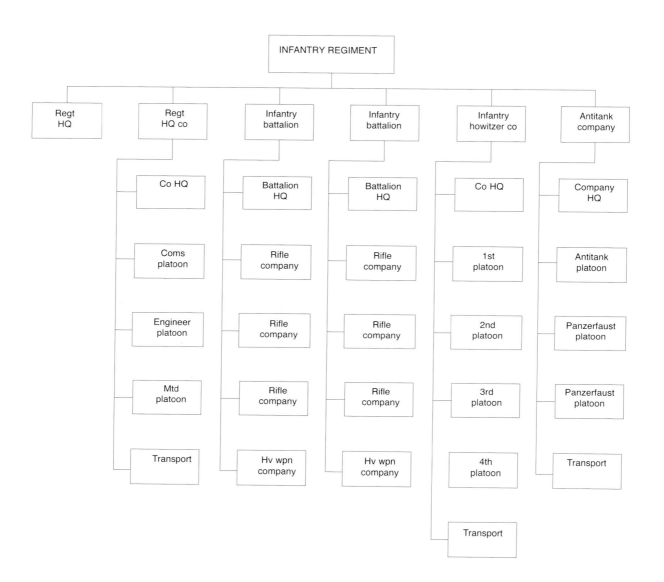

WEHRMACHT INFANTRY DIVISION (1944)

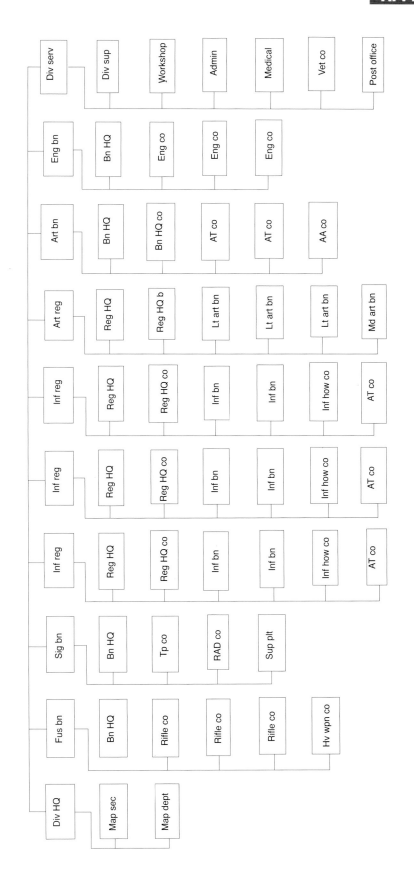

US FIRST ARMY ORDER OF BATTLE
JUNE–AUGUST 1944

V CORPS
2nd Infantry Division
5th Infantry Division
28th Infantry Division

VII CORPS
1st Infantry Division
4th Infantry Division
9th Infantry Division
30th Infantry Division
2nd Armored Division
3rd Armored Division

VIII CORPS
8th Infantry Division
79th Infantry Division
83rd Infantry Division
90th Infantry Division

XIX CORPS
29th Infantry Division
35th Infantry Division

BIBLIOGRAPHY

Primary *(Memoirs)*

Bradley, Omar N., *A Soldier's Story*. Second Edition. (New York: Harry Holt, Inc., 1951; Reprinted New York: Random House, 1999)

Bradley, Omar N., with Blair, Clay, *A General's Life. An Autobiography by General of the Army General Omar N. Bradley*. (New York: Simon & Schuster, 1983; Reprinted: Norwalk, CT: The Easton Press, 1995)

Eisenhower, Dwight D., *Crusade in Europe*. (New York: Doubleday & Company, 1948)

Liddell Hart, B.H. et.al., *The Rommel Papers*. (New York: William Collins Publishers, 1953; Reprinted, Norwalk, CT: Easton Press, 1988)

Montgomery, Bernard Law, *Normandy to the Baltic*. (Boston: Houghton Mifflin Co., 1948)

Montgomery, Bernard Law, *The Memoirs of Field Marshal the Viscount Montgomery of Alamein, K.G.* (Cleveland, OH; World Publishing Co., 1958)

Speidel, Hans, *Invasion 1944. Rommel and the Normandy Campaign*. (Chicago: Henry Regnery Company, 1950)

Standifer, Leon *C., Not In Vain: A Rifleman Remembers World War II*. (Baton Rouge: LA: Louisiana State University Press, 1992)

Official Reports and Studies

Eisenhower, Dwight D., *Report by the Supreme Commander to the Combined Chiefs of Staff on the Operations in Europe of the Allied Expeditionary Force 6 June 1944 to 8 May 1945*. (Washington, D.C., Army Times, Inc., 1945)

U.S. Army Doctrine Combat Development Command, *Evolution of the U.S. Army Division, 1939–1968*. (Fort Belvoir, VA: Combat Operations Research Group, Headquarters, U.S. Combat Development Command, 1969)

U.S. War Department, *Field Service Regulations, Operations May 22, 1941*. Reprinted. (Fort Leavenworth, KS, U.S. Army Command & General Staff College, 1992)

U.S. War Department, *Handbook on German Military Forces*. With an Introduction by Stephen E. Ambrose. (Washington, D.C./Baton Rouge: U.S. War Department/Louisiana State University Press, 1945/1990)

Official Histories

Northern France. The U.S. Army Campaigns of World War II. (Washington, D.C., Center for Military History, 1995)

Omaha Beachhead. (6 June–13 June 1944) (Washington, D.C., War Department: Historical Division, 1945; Reprinted Center for Military History, 1994)

St-Lô. (7 July–19 July 1944) American Forces in Action Series. (Washington, D.C., Historical Section, War Department, 1946; Center for Military History, Government Printing Office, 1994)

Utah Beach to Cherbourg. (6–27 June 1944). (Washington, D.C., Historical Division, 1947; War Department; Center for Military History, Government Printing Office, 1994)

Blumenson, Martin, *United States Army in World War II. The European Theater of Operations. Breakout and Pursuit*. (Washington, D.C., Center of Military History, 1993)

Ellis, L. F., *Victory in the West. Volume I: The Battle of Normandy*. (London: HMSO, 1962)

Harrison, Gordon A., *United States Army in World War II. The European Theater of Operations: Cross-Channel Attack*. (Washington, D.C., Center of Military History, 1989)

Unit Histories

Conquer: The Story of the Ninth Army, 1944–1945. (Washington, D.C.; Infantry Journal Press, 1947)

Third Armored Division Association. *Spearhead in the West. 3d Armored Division in Europe, 1941–1945*. (Frankfurt am Mainz, Schwanheim F.J. Hennich, 1945)

Byrnes, Laurence G., *History of the 94th Infantry Division in World War II*. (Washington, D.C., Infantry Journal Press, 1948)

Hewitt, Robert L., *Work Horse of the Western Front: The Story of the 30th Infantry Division*. (Washington, D.C., Infantry Journal Press, 1946)

Jensen, G. Marvin. *Strike Swiftly: The 70th Tank Battalion: From North Africa to Normandy to Germany*. (Novato: CA: Presidio Press, 1997)

Masters Thesis

Doubler, Michael D., *Busting the Bocage: American Combined Arms Operations in France, 6 June–31 July 1944,* (M.A. Thesis: The Ohio State University, Columbus, Ohio, 1985)

Secondary Sources

Blumenson, Martin, *The Duel For France, 1944. The Men and Battles That Changed the Fate of Europe*. (New York: De Capo Press, 2000)

Brett-Smith, Richard, *Hitler's Generals*. (San Rafael, CA: Presidio Press, 1977)

D'Este, Carlo, *Decision in Normandy*. (New York: Konecky and Konecky, 1994)

Doubler, Michael D., *Closing With the Enemy. How GIs Fought the War in Europe*. (Lawrence, KS: University Press of Kansas, 1994)

Doubler, Michael D., *Busting the Bocage: American Combined Arms Operations in France, 6 June–31 July 1944*. (Fort Leavenworth, Kansas: Combat Studies Institute, U.S. Army Command and General Staff College, 1988)

Fraser, David, *Knight's Cross: A Life of Field Marshal Erwin Rommel*. (New York: HarperCollins, Inc., 1995)

Hart, Stephen Ashley, *Montgomery and "Colossal Cracks": The 21st Army Group in Northwest Europe, 1944–45.* (Westport: Praeger Publishing, 2000)

Hastings, Max, *Overlord. D-Day and the Battle for Normandy.* (New York: Simon and Schuster, 1984)

Howarth, David, *D-Day, The Sixth of June.* (New York: Pyramid Books, 1959)

Levine, Alan J. *From the Normandy Beaches to the Baltic Sea. The Northwest Campaign, 1944–1945.* (Westport: Praeger Publishing Co., 2000)

McManus, John, *The Deadly Brotherhood. The American Combat Soldier in World War II.* (Novato: Presidio Press, 1998)

Messenger, Charles, *The Last Prussian: A Biography of Field Marshal Gerd von Rundstedt, 1875–1953.* (London: Brassey's, 1991)

Murray, Patrick, *Eisenhower versus Montgomery: The Continuing Debate.* (Westport, Praeger Publishing, Co., 1996)

Murray, Williamson, and Millett, Allan R., *A War to Be Won. Fighting the Second World War.* (Cambridge, MA: Harvard University Press, 2000)

Weigley, Russell F., *Eisenhower's Lieutenants: The Campaign of France and Germany, 1944–1945.* (Bloomington: Indiana University Press, 1990)

Weingartner, James J., *Hitler's Guard. The Story of Liebstandarte SS Adolf Hitler, 1933–1945.* (Carbondale: Southern Illinois Press, 1968)

INDEX

PICTURE CREDITS